Read *with* Me

Huron Street Press proceeds support the American Library Association in its mission to provide leadership for the development, promotion, and improvement of library and information services and the profession of librarianship in order to enhance learning and ensure access to information for all.

Read
BEST BOOKS *with* Me
for PRESCHOOLERS

Stephanie Zvirin

an imprint of the American Library Association

HURON STREET PRESS

CHICAGO • 2012

Stephanie Zvirin is an editor for the American Library Association (ALA), where she acquires and develops professional books for ALA Editions and edits ALA Editions' *Children's Programming Monthly* magazine. She was previously Books for Youth editor at *Booklist*, the review journal of the ALA. She is a former teacher and a library director, and is the author of *The Best Years of Their Lives*. Her articles and reviews have appeared in numerous publications, such as *Book Links, Chicago Parent Magazine,* and the *Los Angeles Times.* She lives in Chicago.

Printed in the United States of America
16 15 14 13 12   5 4 3 2 1

Extensive effort has gone into ensuring the reliability of the information in this book; however, the publisher makes no warranty, express or implied, with respect to the material contained herein.

ISBNs: 978-1-937589-03-5 (paper); 978-1-937589-06-6 (PDF); 978-1-937589-07-3 (ePUB); 978-1-937589-08-0 (Kindle).

Library of Congress Cataloging-in-Publication Data
Zvirin, Stephanie.
    Read with me: best books for preschoolers / Stephanie Zvirin.
        pages   cm
    Includes bibliographical references and index.
    Summary: "This authoritative guide—with a core focus on reading readiness and helping position children to succeed in school—offers more than 300 age-appropriate and subject-specific book selections from librarians for reading time with children. From board and picture books to hot new books, these recommendations reflect family, community, play, and the environment. Mirroring a child's world as they grow and mature, chapters include segments on reading together, friendship, places near and far, and making believe. These titles have been culled from the American Library Association's "best" lists and professional review journals"—Provided by publisher.
    ISBN 978-1-937589-03-5 (pbk.)—ISBN 978-1-937589-06-6 (pdf)—ISBN 978-1-937589-07-3 (epub) 1. Preschool children—Books and reading 2. Best books—United States. 3. Reading—Parent participation. 4. Libraries and preschool children. 5. Reading readiness. I. Title.
    Z1037.Z88 2012
    028.533—dc23   2012002405

Book design by Adrianna Sutton using Centaur and Officina Sans typefaces.

♾ This paper meets the requirements of ANSI/NISO Z39.48-1992 (Permanence of Paper).

To my big boys—Michael and Bob

To my colleagues at ALA Publishing, my work family; and
to the many, many librarians whose opinions shaped this book.

CONTENTS

1

READING TOGETHER

WHY READ?

As parents and caregivers, we naturally want to help our children acquire the physical, cognitive, and social skills that will help them in daily life. We show them how to eat with a spoon, tie their shoes, brush their teeth, and put away their toys. By encouraging them to make guided choices, we help them build self-confidence; by supplying them with paper and crayons, we foster their creativity; by visiting the park, we help them develop muscular coordination; by taking them to preschool, a playgroup, or the grocery store, we widen their frame of reference and provide opportunities for them to make friends. We also play a vital role in children's language development. Even before children learn to read and write, they know a great deal about communication—much of which they learn from listening to us as we talk, sing, play with, and read to them. By the time they enter school, they have a vocabulary of between 5,000 and 20,000 words—depending on how much they have been spoken or read to.

It's well established that literacy, the ability to use language in spoken or written form, begins to develop during the first few years of life. The term *early literacy*, often erroneously interpreted to mean "reading," refers to the various overlapping skills that evolve while the brain is undergoing its most rapid growth—between infancy and age five. Multiples studies have shown that repeated exposure to oral language helps strengthen the neural pathways in a child's brain; the more stimuli a child receives, the more connections the brain builds. The more connections, the stronger the foundation for language development, which is the cornerstone of learning and literacy. During these years, children complete a variety of benchmark tasks. For example, they learn that books are opened from left to right, and that there's a difference between pictures and print on a page. They build conversational and listening vocabularies, learn to differentiate small sounds in words, and come to recognize that letters/symbols on the page can relate to spoken words. These facts are strong motivators for sharing books with children early and often.

WHAT TO READ WHEN?

Although every child's needs are different, there are a few important things to keep in mind when choosing books to share. Although infants are largely passive participants in book sharing, they will listen intently for new and different sounds. They may also reach out to touch the books you share with them. Select very short books, with just a few words. Story really doesn't matter; it's the colorful pictures and the sounds that attract Baby's attention. Because an infant's vision is limited to what's right in front of him or her, you should hold the book a little closer than you might ordinarily. Between three and six months, vision evolves sufficiently for babies to track objects. Look for books with pictures of things in a child's everyday world, including pictures of other babies. Point to the images on the page and name them.

During the next year or so children begin to develop preferences. They can usually say a few words, and they'll use them to express their desire for particular persons or objects—like books. Toddlers' attention spans are longer, but books are only one of a long list of interesting things that they want to explore. Books are toys during these months. Little ones throw them, teethe on them, and rip them apart. Board books (easy for busy toddlers to carry around while they investigate their surroundings) work well, as do traditional nursery rhymes and books with simple, catchy verses or sound effects.

By the age of three, most children have a beginning understanding of order and sequence and can follow a picture story that has a beginning, a middle, and an end. Animals are a favorite topic. Also try books that introduce colors, letters, numbers, and opposites. Books with interesting language and predictable, easy-to-memorize refrains are fun, too; after a reading or two, your child may chime right in when you say the words.

Older preschoolers (four- and five-year-olds) will show increased interest in the mechanics of reading. They will bring experiences from their everyday lives and from other books they know to the new stories they hear. They'll often ask questions and make comments, and they'll be more likely to interact with a story on an emotional level. Books about family and friendship are traditionally popular choices because they relate to places, events, or situations children may recognize. At this age many children can recite the words of a favorite book from memory ("Look, I'm reading!"), but most still lack the mechanical and comprehension skills reading demands. By the age of six, children who have had plenty of exposure books and outside stimuli are usually ready and eager to read on their own, and most have gained a healthy, lasting appreciation of books. Your local library is there to help you find whatever you need, whenever you need it.

QUICK TIPS FOR BOOK SHARING

- Reading to infants is as much about bonding and having fun with your child as it is about language and learning.
- Establish a set time for reading each day, but slip in a book whenever it seems practical. Pack a book in your diaper bag; put one in your glove compartment; take a couple to the doctor's office.
- Read with enthusiasm; inflection and tone matter. If you are uncomfortable reading aloud, practice—it's worth it.
- If your child doesn't want to read, don't force the issue. Just try again later.
- Sing some of the words.
- Read slowly. There's more to book sharing than just reciting the words. Reading too quickly prevents your child from talking about the story, which is an excellent way to enhance vocabulary.
- Encourage your prereader if he or she wants to "read" to you for a change.
- Be prepared to read some books over and over. Knowing what happens next in a story helps a child build reading confidence. It also adds to your child's word bank.
- Have an older child read a picture book to a younger sibling—perhaps a picture book that was the older child's favorite.
- Reading an extra book is a great reward, but don't withhold reading to punish a child.
- Books on tender topics—for example, a grandparent's increasing forgetfulness—can ease the way to discussion of real-life situations.

- Try to supplement reading with another activity. Make comments about every new story you share. Ask open-ended questions to encourage conversation.
- Be open to your child's questions, even during the middle of the reading. Questioning is one of the ways children learn about new things and exercise their imaginations.
- Talk about the pictures. Young children look at those first. Only later do children become interested in the words on the page.
- Try sharing wordless books; let your child fill in the story.
- Build a small home library. Include different kinds of books: board books, picture books, easy readers. Organize them in a way that makes sense to your child. Put them in baskets or sort them by color or by size. Keep library books in a special place.
- Make visits to your local library part of your weekly routine.

LIBRARIES, BOOKS, AND MORE

Libraries offer myriad opportunities for your child. Along with books and knowledgeable librarians to help you and your child choose them, you'll find children's audiobooks, DVDs, and CDs, which can be used as reading enrichment. Most public libraries have well-defined, cozy spaces located near their children's book collection, where parents and children can sit, chat, read, or play quietly, and where children can find new friends.

Preschool storytimes are routine in most public libraries. The best are built around parent-child interaction. Open to both parents and caregivers, these programs are often in series that include separate sessions for infants to age six months, toddlers, two- and three-year-olds, four- to six-year-olds, or some similar configuration. Advance registration is usually required, but many libraries also have casual, regularly scheduled drop-in storytimes, some held during the early evening and some right after school. Multiage storytimes (also called *sibling storytimes*) are becoming increasingly popular. These programs comprise activities appropriate for infants as well as their older preschool sibs. They are a very practical alternative for parents or caregivers who have children of different ages. Along with daytime story programs, some libraries have evening sessions, especially during the summer. Children arrive in pj's, and the librarians carefully select the read-alouds and rhymes to serve as a lulling preview to bedtime. More and more libraries are now partnering with bilingual community members to extend storytime opportunities for children and families whose native language is not English.

In addition to the stories, rhymes, songs, flannelboard, and movement activities that make up the usual storytime, many librarians also suggest a craft or additional activity that can be done at home and hand out a list of library books related to their program's theme. They may also integrate early literacy tips and information about school readiness into their storytimes. Passing along information on early literacy is a priority in libraries today. Toward that end, the Association for Library Service to Children (ALSC) and the Public Library Association (PLA), divisions of the American Library Association, have partnered in a research-based initiative designed to equip children's librarians with tools and tactics to help parents and caregivers ready preschoolers for reading and school. Libraries across the country have adopted "Every Child Ready to Read @ your library." Your local library may be one of them. To find out more ask your librarian or visit www.everychildreadytoread.org.

ALSC is also responsible for two of the country's most prestigious children's book awards, the Newbery and the Caldecott, whose winners are chosen by committees comprising librarians from across the country. The Caldecott, first awarded in 1938, honors the artist of the previous year's "most distinguished" picture book. A complete list of award winners is available on the ALSC website www.ala.org/alsc. You will also find a list of Newbery Medal books. This award, for distinguished writing, most often goes to chapter books and novels for older children, though picture books have been among winners. Books for preschoolers and kindergarteners (as well as older children) appear on the following award lists, too, also put together by librarians dedicated to children and books:

Notable Children's Books. The books on this list, which appears each January, are deemed the best children's books published during the previous year. The roundup includes the Newbery and Caldecott medal and honor books along with a wide variety of picture books, and books for middle graders and teen readers to age fourteen.

The (Theodor Seuss) Geisel Awards. Named in recognition of Dr. Seuss's lasting contribution to children's literature, this award goes "to the author(s) and illustrator(s) of the best American book for beginning readers published in English in the United States during the preceding year."

Pura Belpré Medals. These awards recognize the Latino/Latina author and illustrator whose contributions best represent the Latino cultural experience. The award is cosponsored by ALSC and the ALA affiliate

REFORMA, the National Association to Promote Library and Information Services to Latinos and the Spanish-speaking.

The Robert F. Siebert Informational Book Medal. This award, administered by ALSC, recognizes excellent contributions in informational (nonfiction) books. Picture books are eligible.

ALA also supports two other awards that may yield picture book titles to share with your children: the Coretta Scott King Book Awards, which recognize outstanding books for children and teens that have been written or illustrated by African Americans; and the Schneider Family Book Awards, acknowledging an author or illustrator for "a book that embodies an artistic expression of the disability experience for child and adolescent." Learn more and get downloadable lists at www.ala.org/emiert/cskbookawards and www.ala.org/ala/awardsgrants/awardsrecords/schneideraward/schneiderfamily.cfm.

ABOUT THIS BOOK

Librarians too numerous to name chose the books for this volume. Working in big and small public libraries and schools across the country, they put these titles on respected "best books" lists, favorably reviewed them in journals like ALA's *Booklist*, blogged about them, kid-tested them, and used them in storytimes and at home with their own young children.

As any one of them would probably tell you, the age levels suggested for each title in this book are only educated guesses, and the topical arrangement of the book is merely a convenience. Most books are about more than one thing. In addition, what we grown-ups take from a story may be a world away from what a child finds most important or compelling.

You won't find *Goodnight Moon* or *The Snowy Day*, or the *Little Engine That Could* listed in this roundup, even though classics like these are wonderful for sharing. Librarians know them well and can easily steer you toward them. What you *will* find are kid-pleasing books, mostly picture storybooks, published during the last decade. Perhaps they will help your children see the world in a different way, exercise their imaginations, make them curious, or link them to what's going on around them. Like all such lists, this is merely a place to begin. Your local librarian can help you guide your child's book journey.

2

FIRST READS

There is plenty of evidence, both anecdotal and scientific, that babies in utero, in the last stages of development, can hear their mother's heartbeat as well as sounds outside the body. A quick search of the Internet reveals numerous photos of women holding headphones over their bellies so Baby can listen as they read aloud or play music. Babies can hear the bark of the family dog and the home stereo. They can also identify a parent as he or she speaks. Just the sound of a mother's voice can be soothing. It's easy to continue a reading pattern you have established after your newborn arrives. When Baby is able to sit comfortably in your lap, try lap sharing. Just keep in mind that children are nearsighted for the first few months after birth, so hold the book you have chosen close so Baby can see it. Later, as hand-eye coordination develops and Baby becomes more interested in what's going on in the larger world, introduce board books. These books, some small enough for Baby to hold, often center on fundamental learning skills, like counting and colors. They are built for hard use—and they'll get it. Children will carry them around, throw them from the crib, and even chew on them during teething (if you let them). There are also many traditional picture books published for infants and toddlers, some also available as board books. No matter whether you select a board book or a traditional picture book, *first reads* will have minimal text, easy-to-identify shapes without too much detail, brightly colored art, and lots of opportunity for parent-child interaction. Books that call for sound effects from the reader are ideal. The most important thing, of course, is to ensure books become part of your child's life early on.

BOARD BOOKS

10 Little Rubber Ducks
By Eric Carle. Illustrated by the author. HarperCollins, 2005. Ages 1–3.

Ten rubber duckies en route across the ocean in a cargo ship are hurled into a stormy sea. For a time, they bob along together, but eventually they drift apart, each toward a different adventure. The tenth little duck finds a place with some real ducks, and at the end of the book, children are invited to press the rubber duckie's body to hear its satisfied goodnight quack. Carle's books, most of which are available in board book as well as traditional picture book versions, are ideal for helping toddlers learn about colors, shapes, and numbers. Other wonderful Carle titles include *The Very Hungry Caterpillar* and *Brown Bear, Brown Bear, What Do You See?*

Baby Baby Baby!
By Marilyn Janovitz. Illustrated by the author. Sourcebooks, 2010. Ages 1–3.

"Bitsy bouncy baby / On a bumpity lap / Mommy's little baby likes to / CLAP / CLAP / CLAP!" Bouncy rhyme, word repetition, and cheerful pictures of parent-child bonding make this concise catalog of a baby's day a winner. Little ones will see familiar activities in pictures of Baby eating, having a bath, and at the end of the day, slipping off to dreamland. The book also offers lots of opportunity for strengthening coordination as children clap with you.

Baby Shoes
By Dashka Slater. Illustrated by Nakata Hiroe. Bloomsbury, 2006. Ages 2–3.

After donning a pair of new shoes, an irrepressible toddler decides to let his footwear "go, go, go." Leaving the store, he leads his mom on a merry chase. He has a grand time romping and puddle stomping as he races toward home, which predictably transforms his shoes from their original pristine white into all the colors of the rainbow.

A Ball for Daisy
By Chris Raschka. Illustrated by the author. Schwartz & Wade, 2011. Ages 3–5.

This wordless book features a scraggly, energetic little dog named Daisy, who loves to play with her big ball. She chases it, bounces it, puts it on her tummy, kicks it. She even sleeps next to it on the couch. It's her favorite thing in the world. During a visit to the park, tragedy occurs. A bigger dog punctures the ball, sending Daisy into doggie depression. Unlike a child, however, Daisy isn't quite as wedded to her comfort object as it first appears. The arrival of a brand-new ball immediately cures her woes. Children will tell you the story as you look at the book together.

Bear's Birthday

By Stella Blackstone. Illustrated by Debbie Harter. Barefoot, 2011. Ages 2–4.

It's Bear's birthday, and he's throwing a party for himself. He blows up ten balloons to use as favors. His guests join him in games and share a bear-size birthday feast before it's time to go. But that's not all. To complete the story, Blackstone gives little listeners an opportunity to count the balloons from one to ten—while Bear's pugnacious cat leaps across the final pages trying to pop them. Bear appears in many simple, equally charming story books, including *Bear at Home, Bear at Work* and *Bear about Town.*

Dancing Feet!

By Lindsey Craig. Illustrated by Marc Brown. Knopf, 2010. Ages 1–3.

Elephant, caterpillar, bear, lizard, and duck—everyone boogies in this lively book. Italicized words in the text will help adults add zip to their read-aloud. Toddlers will accept the sound effects as an invitation to chime in, while the animal antics might encourage kids to try out their own tippy-tapping. There's no real story; just a cheerful crowd of brightly colored hoofers showing off their "happy, happy dancing feet!" page after page.

Dig Dig Digging

By Margaret Mayo. Illustrated by Alex Ayliffe. Holt, 2002. Ages 2–4.

Some children can never get enough books about cars and trucks. In this peppy roundup, Mayo introduces eleven, from earthmovers to bulldozers "push, push, pushing over rough, bumpy ground." Numerous adjectives and word repetition make this as much fun for grown-up readers as it is for little listeners, and the pictures offer plenty of variety without being overly detailed. What happens to these diligent workers at the end of the day? Just like little children, they quiet their busy "engines" and drift off to sleep.

Global Babies

By the Global Fund for Children. Illustrated with photographs. Charlesbridge, 2007. Ages 2–4.

Babies are fascinated by faces, particularly the faces of other babies. This endearing album is filled with happy baby faces, captured in photos taken in Guatemala, Thailand, Greenland, Mali, the U.S., India, South Africa, Fiji, and elsewhere around the world. Differentiated by colorful costumes or backgrounds, each child looks straight into the camera in a way that connects him or her to the little ones who hold the book in their hands. For a glimpse of babies a bit closer to home, look for *American Babies*, also from the Global Fund for Children.

Go! Go! BoBo Colors

By Simon Basher. Illustrated by the author. Kingfisher, 2011. Ages 2–4.

BoBo, a rambunctious, childlike cartoon character who has appeared in several other concept books, here introduces six colors: red, blue, pink, orange, yellow, and purple. As he skips from page to page, he's treated to a big blob of each color and an array of objects representing the hue: red fire engines, blue butterflies, pink pigs, and so on. The last page brings the colors together in a dazzling rainbow. Children will be primed to look for the colors in their own surroundings. Other BoBo books introduce shapes, numbers, and opposites.

A Good Day

By Kevin Henkes. Illustrated by the author. Greenwillow, 2007. Ages 3–5.

A gentle, reassuring tale that makes real-life challenges understandable to children ready for more complex ideas. Bird sheds a tail feather, a dog's leash becomes tangled, a fox cub is parted from its mother, and a squirrel loses a nut. It appears to be a gloomy day . . . until all the animals discover that their difficulties aren't as bad as they seem. In a winning climax, a child picks up the bird's feather, tucks it behind her ear, and happily declares, "What a beautiful day." The fox, the dog, the bird, and the squirrel agree.

Gossie's Busy Day: A First Tab Book

By Olivier Dunrea. HMH, 2007. Ages 2–3.

Gossie, an endearing yellow gosling, is looking forward to a busy day with sister Gertie, baby brother Ollie, and their friends. Children can join in their play by pulling tabs and lifting flaps in this oversize board book. Other books in the charming Gossie and Friends series get up close and personal with little Ollie; Peedee, who always wears a bright red hat; and BooBoo, easy to spot because he is blue.

Higher! Higher!

By Leslie Patricelli. Illustrated by the author. Candlewick, 2009. Ages 3–4.

An everyday experience gets a clever makeover that could easily be followed by a visit to the playground. "Higher! Higher!" calls the excited little girl to her dad as he pushes her on the swing. "Higher! Higher!" she demands as she soars into the sky, higher than the treetops, higher than a tall building, higher than a mountain—and right into space, where she sees a cloud child swinging downward from above, having an equally good time.

I Go Potty!

By Emily Bolam. Illustrated by the author. Children's Press, 2010. Ages 2–4.

"When I go potty, Bear goes too. / At potty time, there's lots to do." Lots to do? Well, there certainly is enough to keep Bolam's toddler/hippo occupied until it's time to pee. Pants often at half-mast, the little guy plays with his friends and with his special teddy bear, who is right on hand (sitting on a cooking pot) when nature's call sends the little hippo to do personal business on his personal potty.

Little Blue Truck

By Alice Schertle. Illustrated by Jill McElmurry. HMH, 2008. Ages 3–5.

Perfect for tiny truck fans, this offers lots of opportunity for children to moo, neigh, quack, and beep, beep, beep as the story unfolds. Although the road is muddy and full of puddles, a little truck bumps happily along, finding plenty of animal friends as he travels. When he comes across a haughty dump truck in the muck, he stops to help—only to become stuck, too. The animals come to rescue, and soon both vehicles are back on the road, enjoying the scenery.

Little Quack

By Lauren Thompson. Illustrated by Derek Anderson. Simon & Schuster, 2003. Ages 1–3.

Like his larger siblings—Widdle, Waddle, Piddle, and Puddle—chubby Little Quack isn't happy about leaving the safety of the nest for a swimming lesson. Mama Duck is gentle but insistent, and encouraging: "You can do it. I know you can." One by one each duckling takes the plunge, with endearing Little Quack bringing up the rear. A "Quack-U-Lator" runs along the bottom of the page keeping track of the ducklings' progress, at the same time giving children a taste of addition: one duck + one duck + one duck + one duck + one duck equals "five ducklings in the pond."

Look at You! A Baby Body Book

By Kathy Henderson. Illustrated by Paul Howard. Candlewick, 2007. Ages 2–3.

Henderson and Howard bring together an endearing, exuberant cast of babies and toddlers and show what they do best: walk, eat, laugh, play, get dirty, and a host of other activities that children following along in the book will easily recognize. One energetic baby discovers its toes; another splashes happily in its bath.

Max & Ruby's Bedtime Book

By Rosemary Wells. Illustrated by the author. Viking, 2010. Ages 2–4.

Impish rabbit Max and his bossy sister Ruby, who have appeared in more than forty books, continue their sibling rivalry in three bedtime stories told by Grandma. In each story Max manages a small triumph that puts Ruby in her place and makes Grandma smile to herself. Other Max adventures in board book format include *Max's Worm Cake* and *Max's New Suit.*

Mommy Hugs

By Karen Katz. Illustrated by the author. Margaret K. McElderry, 2006. Ages 1–3.

There are plenty of hugs to go around in Katz's celebration of parent-child love and its endearing companion *Daddy Hugs.* "One nuzzle-wuzzle wake-up hug" is only the beginning as Baby doles out a wealth of hugs to Mommy while the two proceed with their day. It's a "yummy hug" at mealtime, a hug at the park, and of course, a snuggly hug when it's time for bed. Katz's illustrations are just as winning as her subject. With their heart-shaped mouths and cherry-colored cheeks, Baby and Mommy are hard to resist. Joanna Walsh's *The Biggest Kiss* is a great follow-up.

My Car

By Byron Barton. Illustrated by the author. Greenwillow, 2001. Ages 1–3.

"I am Sam," begins a tiny driver, who proudly describes features of his fetching red car—a horn that beeps, the purple and green wheels—plus how he cares for it and drives it, watching out for people crossing the street. His destination, a bus, is a sweet surprise: Sam is the bus driver.

My First Soccer Game

By Alyssa Satin Capucilli. Illustrated by Leyah Jensen. Little Simon, 2011. Ages 3–5.

This sturdy board book, meant for children older than the usual board book set, introduces the soccer to wannabe players. Five preschool boys and girls, dressed in soccer uniforms, smile out at readers from the cover photo. Obviously they want to get started. On large foldout pages, they act out what they learn about warming up, stretching, being part of a team, and playing the game.

Oh, Daddy!
By Bob Shea. Balzer & Bray, 2010. Ages 2–4.

Kids know daddies can be oh so silly! Little Hippo's dad is particularly goofy. He can't seem to do anything right; Little Hippo has to show him how to do *everything*. That becomes abundantly clear as father and son make their way through a day's worth of normal activities, from getting dressed and eating to paying a visit to Grandma. Dads don't wear underwear on their head—absolutely not! Dads don't get into the family car through the window—absolutely not! "Oh, Daddy!"

Olivia's Opposites
By Ian Falconer. Illustrated by the author. Simon & Schuster, 2002. Ages 2–4.

Having strutted her stuff in several picture books for older children, child pig Olivia demonstrates her characteristic determination in a series of concept board books. Occasionally eschewing the usual opposites, as befits her prickly porcine personality, Olivia appears "plain" in panties juxtaposed to "fancy" in formal attire and pearls. Her evening dress is long, while her tutu is short. Details in fire-engine red add drama and fun to the freewheeling sketches that show the dynamic pig in action.

Owen's Marshmallow Chick
By Kevin Henkes. Illustrated by the author. Greenwillow, 2002. Ages 3–4.

Little mouse Owen eagerly devours everything in his Easter basket but the marshmallow chick. The chick is the same color as his favorite blankie. The thought of actually eating the chick makes him very uncomfortable—until his practical nature asserts itself, and he finally chomps down. Henkes gets right to the heart a preschooler's feelings here and in other books about mouse characters Sheila Rae, Wemberly, Julius, and Lilly.

Peekaboo Morning
By Rachel Isadora. Illustrated by the author. Putnam, 2002. Ages 2–3.

"Peekaboo! I see . . ." declares a happy toddler in an interactive book about a favorite game. The refrain appears on each left-hand page accompanied by a picture of a charming African American child initiating a game of seek-and-find that she carries on right through her day. Her quarry is everything: Mommy, Daddy, the family dog, and other people and things, which are revealed in turn as the book goes forward.

Planting Seeds

By Nancy Elizabeth Wallace. Illustrated by the author. Marshall Cavendish, 2010. Ages 3–5.

Two simple ideas blend smoothly in this concept book, illustrated in eye-catching paper collages. A lone brown bunny digs a hole; two bunnies plant some seeds; and so on as increasing numbers of bunnies water, nurture, and harvest a crop of carrots all then share: "Ten brown bunnies, 'Time to eat!'" Numerals from 1 to 10, matched to pictures showing corresponding numbers of carrots, allow preschoolers to hone their counting skills, while a final spread serves as visual recap of the bunnies' farming endeavors.

Roadwork

By Sally Sutton. Illustrated by Brian Lovelock. Candlewick, 2008. Ages 2–4.

A delight to read aloud ("Lay the groundwork for the road. / Crash! ROAR! THUMP!"), this book, first published in New Zealand, celebrates how a variety of workers and machines contribute to the building of a road. Endpapers textured to look like asphalt complete the overall effect of a book that combines great information with fun.

Same Same

By Marthe Jocelyn. Illustrated by Tom Slaughter. Tundra, 2009. Ages 3–4.

This clever book takes the idea of grouping a quick step beyond the usual by exploring how completely different things relate: birds fly and so do bees; a bee is striped and so is a zebra. An apple is round and so is the world. Brightly colored objects, stripped of all but essential details, are accompanied by just enough words to start children thinking about the comparisons being made in the artwork. It's a great book for encouraging the very young to think outside the box.

Simms Taback's City Animals

By Simms Taback. Illustrated by the author. Blue Apple, 2009. Ages 2–4.

In a book/guessing game, kids use clues located on a large foldout flap to determine the identities of six big-city animals: a squirrel, a dog, a cat, a horse (as in mounted police), a pigeon, and a mouse. For example: "I gather acorns," reads the first clue. By unfolding the flap children will see a second clue. Another foldout reveals the animal's identity—a squirrel. Sturdy construction will stand up to the multiple readings the book is sure to get. Taback's *Safari Animals* is just as appealing and well made.

Ten Little Fingers and Ten Little Toes

By Mem Fox. Illustrated by Helen Oxenbury. HMH, 2008. Ages 1–3.

A multicultural cast of endearing babies and rhythmic words come together in a joyful book that makes the notions of kinship and tolerance understandable to very young children. Babies may be born a world apart, but "as everyone knows," each baby has ten little fingers and ten little toes. Pictures of chubby appendages and babies toddling across the pages, along with a musical title refrain, ensure repeated readings as well as many occasions to wiggle Baby's fingers and toes.

Ten Tiny Babies

By Karen Katz. Illustrated by the author. Margaret K. McElderry, 2008. Ages 1–3.

Here's another charmingly simple board book from the author of *Mommy Hugs*. This time Katz uses her cherubic babies to initiate counting practice. One tiny baby begins to run, followed by more and more babies having fun—until ten babies, tired from their busy day, fall fast asleep. There are lots of counting books for the age group, but the sunny artwork and bouncy rhyming words distinguish this one. You'll find more babies to look at in *Everywhere Babies* by Susan Meyers, originally published as a picture book, now also available as a large-size board book.

What's Up, Duck? A Book of Opposites

By Tad Hills. Illustrated by the author. Schwartz & Wade, 2008. Ages 2–4.

A little more sedate than *Olivia's Opposites* (above) but equally successful, this nearly wordless concept book enlists the aid of characters from Hill's popular Duck and Goose picture book series to do the work. Duck and Goose demonstrate familiar pairs of opposites, including front and back and high and low. The web-footed friends also appear in concept books on counting and feelings.

TRADITIONAL PICTURE BOOKS
FOR BABIES AND TODDLERS

Apple Pie ABC

By Alison Murray. Illustrated by the author. Disney/Hyperion, 2011. Ages 3–5.

A cut above the traditional alphabet book, this one has a story to support the learning. The teller is a floppy-eared dog, who looks on as his owner, a little girl, makes a pie. Dog eagerly waits while the *a*pple pie *b*akes and *c*ools, and the little girl *d*ishes out a piece for herself. What! No piece for him? The alphabet continues to unfold as the dog figures out a way to *s*teal the treat (*y*um, yum) and ends up catching some *zzzzz*s when he's eaten his fill.

1, 2, Buckle My Shoe

By Anna Grossnickle Hines. Harcourt, 2008. Ages 2–4.

Hines makes use of buttons, plain and printed fabrics, rickrack, and a variety of fancy embroidery stitches in an eye-catching interpretation of the nursery rhyme "One, Two, Buckle My Shoe." The numerals appear in large, quilt blocks, with a roundup of all coming at the end of the book. Endpapers chockablock with brightly colored buttons offer additional opportunities for counting practice.

Baby Face: A Book of Love for Baby

By Cynthia Rylant. Illustrated by Diane Goode. Simon & Schuster, 2008. Ages 1–2.

Little ones will not only see cute babies here (six of them, fetchingly attired in sleepsuits, are lined up on the cover) but also see them involved in familiar activities: naptime, playtime, bathtime, a walk in the park, with all the funny, busy, puzzling moments that happen in between. Everybody loves the babies in this sweet book—even the family dog.

Balancing Act

By Ellen Stoll Walsh. Illustrated by the author. Beach Lane, 2010. Ages 3–5.

Walsh has picked an unusual subject for her concept book. Two mice use a rock and a stick to build a teeter-totter and have a great time playing on it. Trouble starts, though, when other animals of different sizes join in the game. Like *Mouse Paint* and *Mouse Count*, this book gives parents a chance to discuss a bit of simple physics, as well as ideas related to sharing and friendship.

The Big Storm: A Very Soggy Counting Book

By Nancy Tafuri. Simon & Schuster, 2009. Ages 3–5.

As a storm draws near, ten animals look for shelter. The bird is first to take refuge in the cave: "Now there was I. . ." Then Mouse, Rabbit, Chipmunk, and other friends arrive, crowding together as the lightening crackles and the thunder booms outside. When the sun finally returns, the animals pop out to enjoy the rest of the day.

Birds

By Kevin Henkes. Illustrated by Laura Dronzek. Greenwillow, 2009. Ages 3–5.

In this book, a husband-wife team introduces several different concepts at once: color, shape, size, and number. There's even a nod to more sophisticated ideas related to nature. A narrator, not pictured until the end of the story, sees a variety of birds outside her open window. As she talks about their differences, she opens the way for children and parents to look outside and talk about the birds they see in their own backyard.

Choo Choo Clickety-Clack!

By Margaret Mayo. Illustrated by Alex Ayliffe. Carolrhoda, 2005. Ages 3–5.

Here's the perfect book for little ones with a need for speed. Each page pictures a different vehicle and begins in a similarly catchy way: "trains are great at . . ."; "cars are good at . . ."; and so on. The repetition and the rhythm it engenders will easily capture listeners, inviting them to chime right in as each new vehicle is presented. In 2008, the book was introduced as part of the publisher's Touch-and-Feel series, giving children the opportunity to use more of their senses.

Digger Man

By Andrea Zimmerman and David Clemesha. Illustrated by David Clemensha. Holt, 2003. Ages 3–5.

A small boy playing with his toy in the sandbox imagines himself driving the real thing. He moves along, digging, scraping, and crunching rocks and soil until he creates a wonderful park—where he and his brother can play together. Little truck enthusiasts will find this one hard to resist.

Dinosaur vs. the Potty

By Bob Shea. Illustrated by the author. Hyperion, 2010. Ages 2–4.

A little red dinosaur who first appeared in *Dinosaur vs. Bedtime* has found another equally worthy opponent: the potty. No way, no how does he plan to visit one, despite an abundance of liquids in his busy life (three juice boxes for lunch!). "Dinosaur wins again!" he crows after he consumes each liquid. Finally he has no choice but to give in to the urge and allow the potty to win. Both parents and potty trainees will find something to laugh about.

Don't Want to Go!
By Shirley Hughes. Illustrated by the author. Candlewick, 2010. Ages 3–5.

Mommy is sick, and Daddy has to go to work. That means Lily has to spend the day with their pleasant neighbor, Melanie. It's clear from the cover illustration that Lily is angry, worried, and just plain doesn't want to go. It takes a while, but Melanie's baby, Sam, and some attention from Sam's school-age brother and the family dog change her mind, and by the time Dad comes for her at the end of the day, Lily doesn't want to leave. Many children and parents will easily recognize the scenario, and no one will miss Lily's emotional swings, clearly depicted in the art.

Don't You Feel Well, Sam?
By Amy Hest. Illustrated by Anita Jeram. Candlewick, 2002. Ages 2–4.

Wintery winds blow outside as Sam gets ready for bed. All of a sudden, he begins to cough. Mrs. Bear encourages him to down some medicine, but Sam stubbornly refuses. It's only after she promises to let him stay up afterward that he downs the icky stuff. Then the two make tea, snuggle together for stories, and doze by a cozy fire. Brave baby bear Sam makes a worthy model for a sick child.

Duck Tents
By Lynne Berry. Illustrated by Hiroe Nakata. Holt, 2009. Ages 3–5.

The five little ducks from *Duck Skates* and *Duck Dunks* embark on a camping trip. They fish and toast marshmallows before heading off to bed in separate tents. With night noises all around, it isn't long before sleeping apart loses its charm. Written in cheerful rhyming couplets that will be easy to read aloud, this warm, ultimately reassuring story acknowledges that it's okay to feel scared without scaring its audience.

Ella Sarah Gets Dressed
By Margaret Chodos-Irvine. Illustrated by the author. Harcourt, 2003. Ages 3–5.

Young Ella Sarah, a little fashionista, has specific ideas about how to dress. Pink polka-dot pants, striped socks, and yellow shoes seem just fine to her. Unfortunately, her family doesn't think much of her choices. In the end, Ella wins the fashion battle. Her friends arrive for a party, decked out in equally flamboyant ensembles. It's easy to appreciate this gleeful portrayal of a strong-willed child asserting her independence.

Everything I Need to Know Before I'm Five

By Valorie Fisher. Illustrated by the author. Schwartz & Wade, 2011. Ages 3–5.

This wryly comic book takes a cheerful swing at what preschoolers know, using sharp, carefully staged photos filled with things children will easily recognize. The fun begins with the cover photo of a toy dump truck piled high with objects related to concepts children must master before entering school: numbers, opposites, shapes, colors, seasons, weather, the alphabet, and more. Children will find plenty to look at in the pictures and take pleasure in telling Mom and Dad what they've learned as they turn the pages.

Fiesta Babies

By Carmen Tafolla. Illustrated by Amy Córdova. Tricycle, 2010. Ages 3–5.

It's fiesta day. Families celebrate together. The babies have the most fun. They parade through the neighborhood, wearing colorful costumes, dancing, shaking mariachis, eating ("salsa out and salsa in!"), and having a glorious time. After all that activity, could a siesta be far behind? Nope. Spanish terms are sprinkled throughout the story and defined in a glossary at the end of this vibrant book.

First Snow

By Bernette Ford. Illustrated by Sebastien Braun. Holiday House, 2005. Ages 3–5.

Intrigued by newly fallen snow, a little rabbit and its siblings leave Mom in the burrow to see what's going on in the winter-white world at night. Quietly they watch as other animals go about their business, smoke curls from nearby chimneys, and fat snowflakes fall from the sky. They have fun tumbling around in the snow, mimicking children at play. You will feel the crispness of a bright, cold winter's night, even while you and your child sit snugly at home.

The Gobble Gobble Moooooo Tractor Book

By Jez Alborough. Illustrated by the author. Kane/Miller, 2010. Ages 3–5.

When Farmer Dougal sleeps, the farm animals have fun. After all, they reason, what he doesn't know won't hurt him. But being quiet isn't of their plan. As they climb aboard Dougal's tractor, they begin noisily imitating the various sounds the engine makes. "Baa," cries the sheep when the engine starts up, and the other animals follow suit with purrs and quacks and moos and gobbles galore. The energetic warbling wakes Dougal, but by the time he arrives on the scene, everything is quiet. It's easy to see by the innocent-looking expressions on the critters' faces that they have no intention of leaving it that way. Alborough's *Duck in the Truck* and *Fix It Duck* are just as much fun as this book.

Go-Go Gorillas

By Julia Durango. Illustrated by Eleanor Taylor. Simon & Schuster, 2010. Ages 2–4.

King Big Daddy has some very special news, so he summons ten gorilla relatives to join him at his Great Gorilla Villa. Each relative arrives in a different vehicle. One hops in on a pogo stick; one comes on skates; a third arrives in a hot-air balloon. What's the big secret? A baby gorilla. Along with introducing a variety of modes of transportation, Durago substitutes the terms *first, second,* and so on for the usual numerals, demonstrating a new way to count.

Hello, Day!

By Anita Lobel. Illustrated by the author. Greenwillow, 2008. Ages 2–4.

A rooster calls "Cock-a-doodle-doo" to welcome the sun. Other animal voices follow as the day progresses: the cow moos, the sheep bleats, the horse neighs, the duck quacks. "Who-ooo" do you think wishes everyone goodnight? Little listeners will want to join the animal chorus, but the book's softly colored art work makes this a less raucous read-aloud than most barnyard tales; children will participate accordingly.

Hurry! Hurry!

By Eve Bunting. Illustrated by Jeff Mack. Harcourt, 2007. Ages 2–4.

"Hurry! Hurry!" shouts the rooster to his animal friends. From every corner of the barnyard, they race to join him. Why the big rush? An egg is hatching in the barn, and the eager animals want to be present to celebrate the birth and bid the new chick welcome. This is an obvious choice for a sibling in waiting, but it will be a lively read-aloud anytime.

I'm Adopted!

By Shelley Rotner and Sheila M. Kelly. Illustrated with photographs. Holiday House, 2011.
Ages 3–5.

Close-up color photos show many different kinds of adoptive families, while the text addresses common questions adopted children ask their parents as they seek information and reassurance: "Why would my birth mother leave me?" "Why don't I look like you?" Kelly, a psychologist, knows the territory well, and serious issues are nicely balanced by author/photographer Rotner's child-friendly scenarios.

I'm the Best

By Lucy Cousins. Illustrated by the author. Candlewick, 2010. Ages 3–5.

Irrepressible, self-centered Dog loves to compete. Whenever he wins a contest he thoughtlessly proclaims: "I win. I'm the best." His friends find his boasting hard to take, even a little bit mean. After all, Dog can't out dig Mole, even if he runs faster, and although he is bigger than Lady Bug, he's smaller than Donkey. After realizing the hurt he has caused, he apologizes to his friends, who reassure him that he is, in fact, quite special: he has "beautiful fluffy ears." With bright, cheerful artwork and pictures of jovial Dog dancing around on the pages, this book is winner.

A Kitten Tale

By Eric Rohmann. Illustrated by the author. Knopf, 2008. Ages 2–4.

Four curious kittens contemplate the possibilities of winter when they see a picture of a snowy scene. Three worry (after all, it might be cold!), but the fearless fourth "can't wait." When winter finally arrives, he's first out the door, followed by his siblings, who decide they don't want to miss the excitement. Rohmann's feline quartet fairly leaps across the uncluttered pages. Waiting for winter has never been more fun.

La La Rose

By Satomi Ichikawa. Illustrated by the author. Philomel, 2004. Ages 3–5.

La La Rose, a stuffed toy rabbit, is "the inseparable friend of Clementine." But when Grandma takes Clementine and her brother Paris to the playground, La La Rose falls out of her best friend's backpack. Drama ensues in the shape of an encounter with a soccer team and an unpleasant swim in the pond. But little listeners needn't worry. Everything turns out just fine in the end. For a different take on toys lost and found, read Mo Willems's *Knuffle Bunny*.

Little Chicken's Big Day

By Jerry Davis and Katie Davis. Illustrated by Katie Davis. Margaret K. McElderry, 2011. Ages 2–4.

"I hear you cluckin', Big Chicken," says a chick in answer to his mother's instructions—which include the request to stay close when they go out for a walk. Unfortunately, Little Chick misses that instruction; he's already well away, following a butterfly. A few moments of panic ensue when he realizes he's lost. But wise Big Chicken knows her offspring. She's let him go just far enough to learn the lesson. Simple and just plain adorable.

Little One Step

By Simon James. Illustrated by the author. Candlewick, 2003. Ages 3–5.

James's affectionate lesson on patience, perseverance, and family ties centers on three little ducks who have become separated from their mother. The youngest is overwhelmed by the situation, but his siblings devise a simple game called One Step to keep him focused on the long journey ahead of them. He's so good at taking one step at a time that by the time the ducks reunite with Mama he's earned a new name, Little One Step. Young children can identify with the small duck's proud achievement, while their older siblings will get a glimpse of what being a big brother or sister means.

Little Rabbit's New Baby

By Harry Horse. Illustrated by the author. Peachtree, 2008. Ages 3–5.

Little Rabbit wants to be the best big brother in history, but that's harder than he thought. Babies are annoying. They can't do much besides cry and sleep and eat, and they demand constant attention. Regrettably, the babies adore Little Rabbit. What's he to do? In a cozy, lovingly told story that will resonate with both parents and children, Horse mirrors the practical and emotional upheaval children and families deal with when a new baby arrives.

Little White Rabbit

By Kevin Henkes. Illustrated by the author. Greenwillow, 2011. Ages 1–3.

One day while hopping through fields of tall grass and fluffy dandelions, Little White Rabbit wonders what it would be like to be green. After all, turtles and grasshoppers are green. Later, as he hops further along, he considers how it might feel to be tall like a tree or be able to soar through the air like a butterfly. With a sure hand Henkes extends

Little Chicken's Big Day by Jerry Davis and Katie Davis

Little White Rabbit's imaginings, showing him as green as a frog, joyously flapping his long ears alongside the butterflies, and peering over the trees, a giant rabbit looking down at his tiny brethren. The only thing he doesn't wonder about is who loves him, which becomes clear on the very last page.

LMNO Peas

By Keith Baker. Illustrated by the author. Simon & Schuster, Beach Lane, 2010. Ages 3–5.

Baker uses the lowly pea to add some unexpected flavor to the alphabet in this cheerful primer. Each large, colorful letter is surrounded by tiny peas with arms, legs, and faces, who act out the letter being introduced: "We're painters. . . / and plumbers fixing leaks. . . / We're peas and . . . /

We're unique." Having fun with the way most of us string together the letters *L, M, N, O* in the popular alphabet song, Baker presents the letters all together on one funny double-page picture.

Maisy's Book of Things That Go

By Lucy Cousins. Illustrated by the author. Candlewick, 2010. Ages 3–5.

The popular little mouse, the heroine of more than sixty books, takes a break from picture stories to star in a series of informational books for toddlers. In this First Science book, she's the spokesmouse for transportation. Pull tabs add to the attraction of the book, which uses humor to introduce seven modes of transportation. Illustrated sidebars showing items that appear in the main picture serve as parent-child discussion starters. Like all Maisy books, the bright, bold primary colors and thickly outlined shapes call out to kids, as does the cute little mouse with her shiny black nose and pink whiskers.

Mine!

By Shutta Crum. Illustrated by Patrice Barton. Knopf, 2011. Ages 2–4.

Humor is the rule in this virtually wordless book, perfect for encouraging children to fill in the story in their own words. The determined toddler on the cover sets out to best his drooly infant sibling by gathering up all the toys: "Mine!" he loudly declares. Unfortunately for Big Brother, the baby won't cooperate, and neither will the family's playful puppy. Sharing is the operative concept here, and it comes across clearly, even without words.

Mother Goose's Little Treasures

Edited by Iona Opie. Illustrated by Rosemary Wells. Candlewick, 2007. Ages 3–6.

Wells's charming animal and child characters will be familiar to many children and parents. Here they act out twenty-two lesser-known Mother Goose nursery rhymes: "Mrs. Whirly / Mrs. Whirly sells fish, / Three ha'pence a dish; / Don't buy it, / don't buy it, / It stinks / when you fry it." The silliness is contagious. Look for *My Very First Mother Goose* and *Here Comes Mother Goose*, also from Opie and Wells, at your local library; the books also make a great trio for the home bookshelf.

The Neighborhood Mother Goose

By Nina Crews. Illustrated by the author. Greenwillow, 2004. Ages 3–5.

Here's a modern Mother Goose that uses imaginative computer manip-ulated photos of children and grownups in a contemporary Brooklyn neighborhood to capture the fun in the rhymes. Unlike the selections in Opie's collection (above), the rhymes here are familiar ones: "Hush-a-bye, Baby," "Twinkle, Twinkle, Little Star," "The Itsy-bitsy Spider." The overall effect is unusual and compelling. City kids will appreciate the nod to their world; others will find themselves intrigued by familiar rhymes in settings completely different and new.

No

By Claudia Rueda. Illustrated by the author. Groundwood, 2010. Ages 3–5.

The little bear doesn't want to settle down for his long winter sleep and tries his best to convince his mother to let him stay awake. At the same time, his mother tries her best to change his mind, reminding him there won't be any food, and the snow will be cold and deep. He's not too concerned, however, until he realizes he'll be all alone. In very simple terms, Rueda acknowledges children's desire for independence as it coex-ists with their need for love and security.

No More Cookies!

By Paeony Lewis. Illustrated by Brita Granström. Chicken House, 2005. Ages 3–5.

Florence has a problem. She loves cookies to the point where Mom lays down the law: "No More Cookies!" With the help of Arnold, her stuffed monkey, Florence does her best to get around the rule: Arnold has a boo-boo and needs a cookie to survive! Eventually Mom and Flor-ence find common ground: something that satisfies Florence's sweet tooth and also addresses Mom's drive toward healthier snacks. A recipe at book's end will lead parents and kids right to the kitchen.

Oscar's Half Birthday

By Bob Graham. Illustrated by the author. Candlewick, 2005. Ages 2–4.

Oscar is six months old, and his loving interracial family is celebrat-ing with a picnic in the park. The family (mother and father both with braided hair, and sister Milly in her floaty fairy costume) travel to the park. Baby Oscar is, of course, the star of the show. He attracts lots of oohs and ahs from others at the park, all of whom join in lively round of the happy birthday song. Oscar's unabashed joy in it all is contagious. What child wouldn't relish that kind of attention?

¡Pío Peep! Traditional Spanish Nursery Rhymes

By Alma Flor Ada and F. Isabel Campoy. Adapted into English by Alice Schertle. Illustrated by Viví Escrivá. HarperCollins, 2003. Ages 2–5.

With English translations that preserve the poetic flavor of the original verses, this book brings together twenty-nine rhymes that remain popular throughout the Spanish-speaking world. Fingerplays parents can use with their children accompany many of the rhymes. The book is also available with a CD, so children (and parents) unacquainted with spoken Spanish can hear the poems in their original musical language.

A Plane Goes Ka-Zoom!

By Jonathan London. Illustrated by Denis Roche. Holt, 2010. Ages 3–5.

Like *A Truck Goes Rattley-Bumpa* and *A Train Goes Clickety-Clack*, this book uses a few words on a page and a simple rhyme to introduce facts about planes: what they look like (blue or silver), how some fly high and some fly low, and so on. That leaves plenty of room for parent-child discussion of what it's like to fly in one.

Polar Bear Night

By Lauren Thompson. Illustrated by Stephen Savage. Scholastic, 2004. Ages 2–4.

"Something in the moonlit stillness" beckons. A little polar bear cub leaves its warm den to investigate. Kids will accompany the tiny creature as it explores a hushed Arctic world, depicted by Stephen Savage in crisp yet calming shades of blue and gray and white. No glitzy effects here, just minimal text and art to prepare little listeners for sleep.

Press Here

By Hervé Tullet. Illustrated by the author. Chronicle, 2011. Ages 3–5.

Tullet eschews the dye cuts and pull tabs characterizing most interactive books, relying instead on plain colored circles, which strangely enough turn out to be hard to resist. On the first page a colored dot (in this case, it's yellow) invites children to "Press here and turn the page." As they follow subsequent instructions, they'll find themselves rubbing a dot, shaking the book, even blowing on a page. Parents will have just as much fun as their children as they help their kids follow the directions.

Push Button

By Aliki. Illustrated by the author. Greenwillow, 2010. Ages 2–4.

Like his real-life toddler counterparts, the little boy in this book loves to push buttons. Unfortunately, he's mostly oblivious to the consequences. Lights go on, umbrellas pop open, a hose squirts him in the face: "Push button ROARRR! Clean the floor." It's probably a blessing when his button-pushing finger conks out, forcing him to take a break and look for something a little more ordinary to do. The story probably won't convince like-minded toddlers to stop the annoying habit, but parents can always hope.

Red Truck

By Kersten Hamilton. Illustrated by Valeria Petrone. Viking, 2008. Ages 3–5.

"I think I can. I think I can"—a phrase made famous by *The Little Engine That Could*—could easily be the mantra of the red tow truck in this uplifting story. On a wintry day the truck is called out to rescue a school bus stuck in the muck. Other vehicles have tried and failed to climb the slippery hill and extricate the bus. Listeners will feel the tension as the truck accepts the challenge as well as the relief when the work is successfully done.

Sleepy, Oh So Sleepy

By Denise Fleming. Illustrated by the author. Holt, 2010. Ages 3–5.

In the words of a parent lulling a child to sleep, this tender bedtime book links the tiny baby on the cover to other sleepy animal: "Tiny baby panda, / sleepy, oh so sleepy. / Tiny baby ostrich, / sleepy, oh so sleepy." On each double-page spread, a different animal parent watches as its baby closes its eyes and drifts off to sleep. The focus momentarily shifts to human babies, then broadens to encompass sleeping little ones across the world. A soothing tale, certain to make parents yawn and send little ones off to untroubled dreams.

Stretch

By Doreen Cronin. Illustrated by Scott Menchin. Atheneum, 2009. Ages 3–5.

The flop-ear canine who wiggled and bounced his way through two previous picture books (*Wiggle* and *Bounce*) is on the move again, this time in what might seem to be a less taxing activity. Wrong. Dog manages to be just as vigorous as before as, decked out in a leotard, he leads a yoga class, rides the waves stretched out on a surfboard, watches as his bubble gum bubble gets bigger and bigger, and more—managing to prove that the more you put into something, the more you get out of it. The words stretch out, shrink, or tilt on the page according to Dog's particular activity. All three books are clear invitations for kids to limber up and get moving.

Ten Little Caterpillars

By Bill Martin Jr. Illustrated by Lois Ehlert. Beach Lane, 2011. Ages 2–4.

All new art gives Martin's jaunty, rhyming text, first published in 1967, an updated, more colorful look. Ten different kinds of caterpillars wiggle their way through a lovely garden: the first crawls "into a bower"; the next, up the stalk of a flower, and so on. The main text appears in large print on the page; smaller print is used to identify the various animals and plants that fill the garden. The closing picture shows all the caterpillars and the butterflies and moths they eventually become.

There's Going to Be a Baby

By John Burningham. Illustrated by Helen Oxenbury. Candlewick, 2010. Ages 2–4.

"There's going to be a baby," a mother tells her son, a declaration prompting all sorts of questions from the boy. When will the baby come? What's the baby's name? The answers, straightforward though they are, never quite hit home, which leaves the sibling-to-be speculating wildly about his new brother or sister. The obviously close relationship between mother and son (no father appears in the book) will comfort young listeners who face similar changes in their family.

Truck Driver Tom

By Monica Wellington. Illustrated by the author. Dutton, 2007. Ages 3–5.

Traveling along a road, up hills, and over bridges and train tracks, a busy trucker, accompanied by his dog, drives his big rig from the farm to the city. Along the way he encounters nearly fifty vehicles—from large to small, from fast to slow. Allow plenty of time for children to peruse the illustrated roundup of vehicles at the end of the book, decide which ones they like best, and go back to the story to find them on the roadway. The bold colors of the pictures make this field guide for drivers-in-the-making just about perfect.

What Brothers Do Best/What Sisters Do Best

By Laura Numeroff. Illustrated by Lynn Munsinger. Chronicle, 2009. Ages 2–4.

The author and the illustrator who created *What Mommies Do Best/What Daddies Do Best*, What *Grandmas Do Best/What Grandpas Do Best*, and similar books about other relatives continue their focus on family in back-to-back appraisals of brothers' and sisters' activities. The talents of siblings are applauded in simple sentences and demonstrated in pictures of adorable animal pairs. A big sister can teach you how to play soccer or climb a tree. A big brother can teach you how to swim. Who can do what isn't the important thing here. What counts is the admiration and devotion that underlies all.

What If?

By Laura Vaccaro Seeger. Illustrated by the author. Roaring Brook/Neal Porter, 2010.
Ages 3–5.

In three very simple related scenarios, Seeger depicts the pain of being left out. In the first one a brown seal and a gray seal are playing with a ball. What if a purple seal wants to join and the brown seal is left out? The second one poses the question "What if the purple seal is left out? The book ends on a happy note: What if everyone plays together?

What James Likes Best

By Amy Schwartz. Illustrated by the author. Atheneum, 2003. Ages 3–5.

Four brief stories follow toddler James when he goes visiting. In the first one he travels by bus to see a family with twins. Next he takes a taxi to Grandma's. After that he rides with his parents to a county fair, and last but not least, he visits his friend who lives down the block. Then comes Schwartz's question "What do you think James liked best?" Prepare for some great parent-child discussion about traveling, how to have fun, and making choices.

What Puppies Do Best

By Laura Numeroff. Illustrated by Lynn Munsinger. Chronicle, 2011. Ages 2–3.

In this collection of unrelated scenes, dogs do what they do best: play with kids. Puppies give children sloppy kisses to wake them; they sit when asked (sometimes) and run around (a lot). They love to play with balls and with one another, and they snuggle up with kids at the end of the day. The cute pictures do the heavy lifting here; there are only five or six words on each page. Include this in your read-aloud library anyway. It's a good choice for new readers to read aloud to younger siblings. You can simply sit by and enjoy the goings-on.

Where Is the Green Sheep?
By Mem Fox. Illustrated by Judy Horacek. Harcourt, 2004. Ages 2–4.

Little ones will quickly catch on to the rhythm of Fox's text and be eager to yell, "Where is the green sheep?" at the turn of each page. The pictures make the rounds of a flock as everyone looks for the green sheep. There's a red sheep, a blue sheep, romping sheep, singing sheep—all kinds of sheep, *except* the green sheep. It doesn't appear until the very last page, where children will finally spot it, snoozing away under a bright green bush.

Zoo Day ¡Olé! A Counting Book
By Phillis Gershator. Illustrated by Santiago Cohen. Marshall Cavendish, 2009. Ages 3–5.

Gershator's bilingual picture book combines a charming story with a counting lesson in English and Spanish. A preschooler talks about counting the animals she sees at the zoo during a trip with her brother and grandmother. Each page offers little ones a look at how the numbers appear written out in both languages as well as several opportunities to count along with the narrator. At the end of the journey/story, there's a picture showing all the animals the trio saw on their outing. When it's time to go to bed, Abuelita gives the children *dos besos,* two kisses, to carry them off to sleep.

3

ME, ME, ME

As children's attention spans increase and they are able to listen to more intricate stories, they start making connections between the characters and events in a book and what's happening in their everyday lives. The picture books in this chapter, which are longer and more complicated than first reads, address everyday routines and feelings—longing for a pet, moving away, testing limits, finding a special talent, experiencing new things, feeling happy, being sad. Animal characters substitute for children in many of these books, giving listeners a little extra space to think through what the story says to them.

All in a Day
By Cynthia Rylant. Illustrated by Nikki McClure. Abrams, 2009. Ages 4–6.

A positive message about opportunity and the value of life runs through a book that follows along as a farm boy feeds the chickens, helps in the garden, explores the fields, and naps in the warming sun. The intricate illustrations, cut from black paper and mounted on gold and blue backgrounds, add a retro feel to the contemplative story, which reflects "a perfect piece of time to live a life." Try reading this at the end of a busy day.

Baby Brains
By Simon James. Illustrated by the author. Candlewick, 2007. Ages 4–6.

According to everyone, including himself, Baby Brains is the smartest baby in the world. He handles his extraordinary abilities with compo-

All in a Day by Cynthia Rylant

sure until he is sent into space. While free-floating miles above Earth, he concludes that being home and doing things other babies do may not be so bad after all. James provides proof that there's no place like home. Read more about the toddling Einstein in *Baby Brains and Robomom* and *Baby Brains Superstar.*

A Beach Tail

By Karen Lynn Williams. Illustrated by Floyd Cooper. Boyds Mills, 2010. Ages 4–7.

Gregory, an African American boy who wants to explore the beach, is sternly reminded to stay near the picture of the lion he has drawn in the sand. Bored, the child occupies himself by using his stick to draw a tail on the beast. By extending the tail farther and farther, he manages to explore his surroundings without technically disobeying the order. Before he knows it, however, he has gone so far he can't even see Dad's beach umbrella. After a few moments of panic, he knows just what to do. He follows the zigzagging trail of the lion's tail right back to its beginning. Whether the topic is testing limits or creativity, this ultimately reassuring story opens the way for parent-child discussion.

Bella and Stella Come Home

By Anika Denise. Illustrated by Christopher Denise. Philomel, 2010. Ages 4–6.

Moving to a new house turns a little girl's life topsy-turvy, but she learns to cope with the help of her imagination. Bella is lucky; she has Stella, her stuffed elephant friend, to keep her company. When Bella is worried, Stella grows to into a giant, becoming Bella's faithful elephant protector. When Bella is curious and calm, Stella is a small, cuddly, stuffed-toy pal. Together, they can handle anything. Libby Gleeson's *Clancy and Millie and the Very Fine House* is another good story about how a family's move can affect a child.

Buster

By Denise Fleming. Illustrated by the author. Henry Holt, 2003. Ages 4–6.

Buster the dog is king of the castle until his (certainly misguided) owner brings an interloper into the house. Betty, a cat, makes herself right at home, leaving Buster both a tiny bit fearful and more than a little put out. She steals his toys! Twiddling with his favorite radio station is the last straw for Buster. He runs off to the park to blow off some steam— only to forget how to find his way home. Guess who comes to the rescue. Don't miss the map showing Buster's route.

Caramba

By Marie-Louise Gay. Illustrated by the author. Groundwood, 2005. Ages 4–6.

Cats can fly—all cats except Caramba. He's as earthbound as his friend Portia the Pig. Unwilling to admit his difficulty, he practices in secret. When cat cousins Bijou and Bug find out, they help him test his progress by dropping him off a cliff. Unfortunately, Caramba still can't fly— but to his delight, he discovers he can swim. Gay has written a variety of equally charming picture books, including *Stella, Queen of Snow,* and *What Are You Doing, Sam?*

Buster by Denise Fleming

Celestine, Drama Queen
By Penny Ives. Illustrated by the author. Arthur A. Levine, 2009. Ages 4–6.

Celestine is no ordinary duckling. She's convinced she's bound for stardom, and she's thrilled when her teacher announces a class play. When the time to act comes, however, she suffers such a case of stage fright she can't say her part. Mrs. Gobble comes to the rescue by playing a lively tune, which helps Celestine take another swing at stardom. Although her stage debut isn't quite what she hoped, Celestine knows that to Mama Duck she will always be a star. Celestine is Everychild in feathers.

Children Make Terrible Pets

By Peter Brown. Illustrated by the author. Little, Brown, 2010. Ages 4–6.

In a whimsical twist on a familiar family scenario, a little girl bear, Lucy, wants a child for a pet. Almost like magic she finds one in the forest. Mother Bear warns, "Children make terrible pets," but Lucy is unconvinced. Squeakers, as she calls him, will be different. He's not. He wreaks havoc on the household and proves less than cooperative when it comes to potty training. What's a pet owner to do? The problem is soon solved, with a happy ending that comes with a message that having a pet isn't all fun and games. In Fiona Roberton's *Wanted: The Perfect Pet*, a duck sets out to convince a little boy that a duck can be the ideal pet companion.

David Gets in Trouble

By David Shannon. Illustrated by the author. Scholastic, 2003. Ages 4–7.

Shannon's previous books about unruly David were about a child testing limits of behavior. This one is about making excuses. That's just what David does, whether at home or at school. "But she likes it!" he says while pulling the cat's tail; "But Dad says it!" he mumbles around bubbles from the bar of soap in his mouth. Each hapless act begets a different excuse, but there's hope for the future when he owns up at the end of the day. Both parents and children will find a lot that rings true in David's story.

The Dot

By Peter H. Reynolds. Illustrated by the author. Candlewick, 2003. Ages 5–7.

Vashti doesn't like art class because she thinks she can't draw. When her teacher insists she participate, Vashti stubbornly makes a single dot on the paper and hands it in. Seeing her picture on the wall convinces her she can do better, and soon she's experimenting and having all kinds of fun. An important message wrapped in a tidy package.

Edwin Speaks Up

By April Stevens. Illustrated by Sophie Blackall. Schwartz & Wade, 2011. Ages 4–7.

Baby Edwin, the youngest in the Fennimore ferret family, accompanies his mother and rowdy siblings to the grocery store to get sugar for his birthday cake. One thing after another goes awry. Calmly observing the goings-on from his seat in the grocery cart, Edwin sees the mishaps in the making, but his warnings go unheeded; his family can't understand his baby jibber jabber ("Clob foo Poop SWEETY"). Sharp-eyed kids following the pictures will realize that they know more than the family when it comes to Edwin's oratory. They'll even figure out his babbled reminder not to forget the sugar, which, at the end of the story, is shown teetering on the roof of the speeding family car.

Faith

By Maya Ajmera, Magda Nakassis, and Cynthia Pon.
Illustrated with photographs. Charlesbridge, 2009. Ages 5–7.

Created by the Global Fund for Children, an organization dedicated to helping children understand and accept the importance of diversity, this striking photo essay pictures young people practicing their faith in thirty-seven countries around the globe. From pictures of a Taoist child in Hong Kong and Muslim children in Saudi Arabia to a young Christian girl in the United States, the photos tug at the heartstrings. At the same time they depict the different ways faith can be expressed— through chanting, praying, celebrating holy days, feasting, and mentoring and teaching others. The selection of images is diverse, but the message of the book is one of community rather than separateness. A few words of background accompany each crisp, full-color photo, and a map identifying the countries mentioned in the text provides more for parents and children to talk about.

Fox

By Kate Banks. Illustrated by Georg Hallensleben. Farrar Straus Giroux, 2007. Ages 4–6.

Here's a soothing celebration of growing up and, with parents' loving help, becoming independent. The passing seasons mark the changes in the life of a little fox. Born in winter, it snuggles with its parents, safe in the den. In spring, it grows curious and yearns to explore outdoors. In summer it is big enough to hunt, and when the leaves begin to fall, it is ready to strike out on its own. A quiet and warmly told tale about the certainty of change—for foxes, of course, but also for children.

Harry & Hopper

By Margaret Wild. Illustrated by Freya Blackwood. Feiwel and Friends, 2011. Ages 4–7.

Harry, a boy, and Hopper, a dog, are inseparable, and when Hopper is killed in an accident, Harry is inconsolable. At night Hopper appears in

Harry's bedroom, and the two play together again. Hopper returns each night (is it a dream?) until he senses that Harry is ready to let him go. This tender story acknowledges children's deep attachments and their feelings about love and loss in a way young readers will understand.

I Can Be Anything!

By Jerry Spinelli. Illustrated by Jimmy Liao. Little, Brown, 2010. Ages 4–6.

Spinelli offers a fresh and charming take on a common theme. In rhyming phrases, a young boy considers: "When I grow up, what shall I be? / Of all the many, many jobs, which one will be the best for me?" Doctor and lawyer never cross his mind. Instead, he's thinking about becoming a pumpkin grower, a dandelion blower, and a silly-joke teller—things he might want to undertake without the fuss of actually growing up. Energetic art shows him giving each one a try. In the end, he's had so much fun he's prepared to do them all.

I'll Be There

By Ann Stott. Illustrated by Matt Phelan. Candlewick, 2011. Ages 4–6.

In a warm, gentle story that speaks to the mother-child bond, a little red-haired boy struggles with his desire for independence and his love and attachment to his mother. During a walk, the child talks to his mother about his babyhood, which she fondly recalls. She fed him, bathed him, and dressed him, and lots of other things the boy can now do on his own—thanks to his mother's patience and enduring love coupled with his own desire to grow up.

I'm Getting a Checkup

By Marilyn Singer. Illustrated by David Milgrim. Clarion, 2009. Ages 4–6.

A heartening view of a visit to the doctor's office for a checkup, with cartoon art showing three children (parents nearby) being weighed, measured, and checked "from neck down to neck up." While the children describe doctors and nurses going about their routines, a second layer of text explains in simple terms some of the equipment at a modern doctor's office: "I'm still a little scared. / But knowing what each tool is for helps me feel prepared." The information, the gentle humor, the smiling faces of parents and doctors, and the acknowledgment of a child's anxieties will help prepare children for a routine experience.

I'll Be There by Ann Stott

Jibberwillies at Night

By Rachel Vail. Illustrated by Yumi Heo. Scholastic, 2008. Ages 4–6.

In *Sometimes I'm Bombaloo* (below), Katie Honors learned how to handle angry feelings. This time it's jibberwillies—worrisome flying creatures who show up at night when the lights go out. She tries to be tough, but she can't quite manage without Mom, who finds a great solution to Katie's night fright: she and Katie gather the offending jibberwillies in a bucket and fling them out the window. Among the many books on the topic, this one does more than acknowledge apprehensions; it offers a surprisingly practical way that might put them to rest.

Jumpy Jack & Googily

By Meg Rosoff. Illustrated by Sophie Blackall. Holt, 2008. Ages 4–6.

Jumpy Jack the snail can't manage on his own. Because he's afraid of just about everything (especially monsters) he has his buddy Googily reconnoiter. Googily looks in the yard, in the house, everywhere. That Googily happens to be a monster is part of the joke, though Googily's obvious devotion to Jack and his jaunty bowler and orange umbrella make him more comical than scary. "What if a monster stares at me through the letterbox?" asks Jack, whose buddy does that very thing. Kids will love being more in-the-know than the story's characters.

Katy Did It!
By Lorianne Siomades. Illustrated by the author. Boyds Mills, 2009. Ages 4–6.

Katydid Katy's younger brother, Lou, who follows her everywhere, is a tattler. When energetic Katy, who loves to jump, accidentally scatters the bumblebee's pollen and tangles the spider's web, Lou is quick to call out, "Katy did it!" But when Katy comes to the rescue of some ants, Lou changes his tune if not his words; "Katy did it," he cries, this time alerting everyone to how she saved the day. It's an unusual child who hasn't tattled; try using this book to start a conversation on the subject.

Knuffle Bunny Free: An Unexpected Diversion
By Mo Willems. Illustrated by the author. Balzer & Bray, 2010. Ages 4–6.

The quizzical, flop-eared toy rabbit that first appeared with toddler Trixie in *Knuffle Bunny* has been around the block a time or two since being rescued from the laundromat. He's a bit grubbier than he was in the old days. Trixie has changed, too. She's growing up. When she accidentally leaves her old friend on an airplane, she's very sad. She doesn't love him less—but she doesn't need him anymore. Children worried about what happens to the faithful bunny will like the touching four-page foldout that gives the rabbit a new lease on life.

Ling & Ting: Not Exactly the Same!
By Grace Lin. Little, Brown, 2010. Ages 4–7.

Chinese American sisters Ling and Ting are twins, and everyone tells them they are just alike. They do look identical—until the barber trims too much off Ting's bangs. That makes it much easier to tell which twin makes lumpy dumplings and which can't master chopsticks. Lin is also the author of *Dim Sum for Everyone!* and *Fortune Cookie Fortunes.*

Llama Llama Home with Mama
By Anna Dewdney. Illustrated by the author. Viking, 2011. Ages 4–6.

Llama feels "yucky, just not right!" He's sneezy and wheezy, and his throat hurts. No school for him today, says Mama Llama. He'll stay home in his red pajamas (the same ones he wears in *Llama Llama Red Pajama*) while Mama nurses his coughs and sneezes. She feels his forehead, straightens his covers, and brings him books to read. Just when he starts feeling better, Mama begins to sneeze. Now little Llama will take care of Mama. The latest book in a popular series certainly proves that love is the best medicine.

Lizette's Green Sock

By Catharina Valckx. Illustrated by the author. Clarion, 2005. Ages 3–5.

Children independent of mind when it comes to their wardrobes are the perfect audience for this tender book. On a walk one lovely day, Lizette (a little bird) finds a lone green sock. Pleased with her unusual find ("You don't find a beautiful sock like this every day!"), she puts it on and continues happily on her way. Her good humor evaporates, however, when she's told that socks are meant to be worn in pairs. It's restored when her friend demonstrates another use for the sock: it makes quite a wonderful hat.

Looking Like Me

By Walter Dean Myers. Illustrated by Christopher Myers. Egmont, 2009. Ages 5–8.

Dynamic contemporary art that crackles with energy couples with rhythmic, raplike verse, perfect for reading aloud. With special resonance to boys, the book is more portrait than traditional story. As young Jeremy travels through Harlem, he encounters a number of people whose lives he has touched—his sister, his father, his teacher, his grandmother. Their simple, positive affirmations of his role in their lives make him feel proud and strong. Simple enough for young children, and thoughtful enough to read with older ones.

Lottie Paris Lives Here

By Angela Johnson. Illustrated by Scott M. Fisher. Simon & Schuster, 2011. Ages 4–6.

African American Lottie is a happy, curious child. She loves running around outdoors or imagining she's a princess who lives in a toy castle. She always finds something interesting to do, even if her actions occasionally get her in trouble. Her special fondness for her father, whom she calls Papa Pete, comes through on every page—whether she's testing his limits or playing funny tricks they both enjoy. Like Emily Jenkins's *What Happens on Wednesdays*, this is a charming portrait of a contented child.

Lucy and the Bully

By Claire Alexander. Illustrated by the author. Albert Whitman, 2008. Ages 4–6.

Bullying is an increasingly widespread problem, not only in schools but also on playgrounds and neighborhoods across the country. In this book Lucy, a little lamb, is being bullied by her classmate, a bull named Tommy. He sabotages her artwork and makes fun of her. Their teacher is oblivious. Trouble escalates, and when Lucy decides she can't manage alone, she tells her mother. When her mother calls the teacher, who in turns calls Tommy's parent, Lucy is horrified. But the next day Tommy looks so sad that Lucy swallows her fear and takes the initiative to pay him some attention. Bullying is rarely put to rest so simply, but Lucy's fictional experience may encourage little ones under similar stress to enlist their parents' help, and the lamb's willingness to forgive her tormenter is well worth discussing. A follow-up note to parents suggests other ways to help a struggling child. *The Recess Queen* by Alexis O'Neill is another good book for sharing.

My Name Is Yoon

By Helen Recorvits. Illustrated by Gabi Swiatkowska. Farrar Straus Giroux, 2003. Ages 5–7.

Yoon, newly arrived in America, is having a difficult time adjusting. Her name, which means "shining wisdom" in Korean, doesn't seem to fit now; it's much more suited to the wonderful place she has left behind. Her teacher encourages her to practice writing her name in English, but Yoon resists, substituting other words like *cupcake* and *bird*, which seem to better fit her new life. Her parents' and teacher's gentle encouragement eventually win her over, and in the end, she writes her name both ways.

No Two Alike

By Keith Baker. Illustrated by the author. Beach Lane, 2011. Ages 4–7.

On a wintery day two little red birds have fun in the snow. They make tiny snowballs, transform pine needles into skis, and tickle a sleepy squirrel's nose with a feather. As they play they observe differences in the things that surround them: the squirrel's nest differs from the bird's nest; the pine needle tracks are different lengths; some snowflakes are big and some are small. Even the two birds, who at first glance look so much alike, aren't quite the same: "Are we the same—just alike? / Almost, almost . . . but not quite." Children will want a close-up look at the tiny birds when the story has ended.

No Two Alike by Keith Baker

Not Afraid of Dogs

By Susanna Pitzer. Illustrated by Larry Day. Walker, 2006. Ages 4–6.

Daniel has a problem; he's afraid of dogs, and he hasn't told a soul. When his aunt's dog Bandit comes to stay, Daniel goes into hiding. After discovering both he and Bandit are afraid of thunderstorms, he decides Bandit isn't all that bad. At the end, he even lets Bandit sleep in his bed.

Not All Princesses Dress in Pink

By Jane Yolen and Heidi E. Y. Stemple. Illustrated by Anne-Sophie Lanquetin.
Simon & Schuster, 2010. Ages 4–6.

Princesses and little girls just seem to go together. That doesn't mean girls can't play soccer, get dirty, wear bike helmets—or refuse to wear pink. Putting stereotypes to rest, this vibrant book makes it clear that little girls (and little boys, for that matter) are more than one thing. Pictures showing girls in jeans and jerseys with princess crowns on their head make the case admirably.

Orange Pear Apple Bear

By Emily Gravett. Illustrated by the author. Simon & Schuster, 2007. Ages 3–5.

A brown bear is the facilitator in this comical book that jokes around with shape, color, words (only five words appear in the story), and pieces of fruit. It's hard to resist the yummy fruit, but the bear doesn't eat it straightaway. He stacks it on his head, juggles it, balances it on his paw, and so on. It's almost a shame when he eats his lovely toys, but by that time little ones will have had plenty of opportunity to appreciate the wordplay and imagine their own bear backstory.

The Pirate of Kindergarten

By George Ella Lyon. Illustrated by Lynne Avril. Atheneum/Richard Jackson, 2010.
Ages 4–6.

Lyon drew on his own experience when he wrote this story about a child with vision problems. Ginny likes kindergarten, but her classmates occasionally laugh at her when she runs into chairs or makes mistakes when she reads. On vision screening day, the school nurse discovers that Ginny has double vision. To correct it, the doctor gives her an eye patch, which Ginny uses to turn herself into "Kindergarten Pirate." The other kids think pirates are soooo cooool!

Princess K.I.M. and the Lie That Grew

By Maryann Cocca-Leffler. Illustrated by the author. Albert Whitman, 2009. Ages 4–6.

Kim is anxious to fit in at her new school, so instead of telling classmates she's just plain Kim, she introduces herself as Princess K.I.M., Katherine Isabella Marguerite. It's not entirely a lie, she thinks; Daddy calls her "Princess." With the exception of skeptical Jonathan, her classmates are suitably impressed. She gets more attention than she knows what to do with. Then Grandma Betty comes to the class. Kim is sure she'll be exposed, but wise Grandma plays along—giving Kim an opportunity to clear up her own mess. In the end, Kim does come clean. She also realizes she likes being just plain Kim, especially since at least one classmate, Jonathan, respects her courage in telling the truth. Kids will recognize not only the strong temptation to tell a lie when things get tough, but also the relief when the truth comes out.

The Quiet Book

By Deborah Underwood. Illustrated by Renata Liwska. Houghton Mifflin, 2010. Ages 4–6.

The Loud Book!

By Deborah Underwood. Illustrated by Renata Liwska. Houghton Mifflin, 2011. Ages 4–6.

Talk about opposites! Using the same cast of small animals in both these books, Underwood and Liwska thoroughly investigate the flip sides of sound as related to a child's world. In *Quiet* animals are pictured in solitary activities, playing contentedly with friends and being with family. There's also the silence of a new snowfall, the stillness of a dark theater, and the quiet that comes when someone is sad or has done something naughty. There are lots of louds in *Loud*—sounds children hear but rarely think about (someone unwrapping candy in the movies) as well as happy, funny more everyday sounds, such as whistling and cheering. When it comes to burping, expect audience participation.

Ready for Anything!

By Keiko Kasza. Illustrated by the author. Putnam, 2009. Ages 4–6.

Adventurous Duck and his anxious friend Raccoon are planning a summer outing. Raccoon imagines the worst: a dreadful storm, bees, a terrifying dragon living in a cave. He scares himself so much he hides. Duck's imagination conjures a more comforting scenario: a lovely lake instead of pouring rain, butterflies instead of bees, a cool, quiet cave where a baby dragon lives. His version soothes his uneasy friend, who decides he'll go on the picnic—but he takes a flashlight along just in case. Duck is a good enough buddy not to care.

Saying Goodbye to Lulu

By Corinne Demas. Illustrated by Ard Hoyt. Little, Brown, 2004. Ages 4–6.

A little girl cares deeply for her elderly dog, Lulu, but she knows that Lulu isn't able to play as she once did, and that one day soon Lulu will die. Even though the beloved dog's death is expected, it takes some time before the girl can say good-bye. As the story ends, she gets a puppy, and realizes that she has the capacity to love both her dear old friend and her sweet new one.

Shades of People

By Shelley Rotner. Illustrated by Sheila M. Kelly. Holiday House, 2009. Ages 4–7.

"Our skin is just our covering, like wrapping paper. And you can't tell what someone is like from the color of their skin." The message here is both obvious and charming. The story is in the upbeat photos that parents and children can look at together. Candid shots as well as posed ones show children with skin fresh as peaches, rich as cocoa, and everywhere between, playing and laughing together, at home and at school. The question sure to follow: "Which shade am I?"

Small Saul

By Ashley Spires. Illustrated by the author. Kids Can, 2011. Ages 4–6.

No doubt about it: Saul is small—too small, it seems, to join the navy. "Fortunately, pirates aren't so picky," but Saul isn't great pirate material. He bakes, loves sea shanties, and is great at fixing boo-boos, but he's lousy at looting and hunting for treasure. He also has a bunny tattoo on his arm. He drives his pirate pals nuts. When the captain pushes him overboard, everyone rejoices—until the tough guys miss their cookies. They also miss Saul, who is kind enough to forgive them when they return to scoop him up: "After all, throwing people overboard is just something [pirates] do." Lots of fun, as well as a gateway to discussing forgiveness and being oneself.

Sometimes I'm Bombaloo

By Rachel Vail. Illustrated by Yumi Heo. Scholastic, 2002. Ages 4–6.

As she does in *Jibberwillies at Night* (above), Vail gets right inside a child's head, this time in a book about coping with anger. Katie Honors usually follows the rules and manages her busy life with aplomb; she even gets on with her little brother. But every once in a while, when she can't cope with her sibling or something goes wrong, she becomes "Bombaloo." She stamps her feet and yells, and hates everybody and everything. Her mother sends her to her room, where she throws her toys and clothes. When her underpants land on her head, she laughs, and suddenly, "I'm Katie Honors again." This is more than a book about a child having a tantrum. It's clear from the pictures that Katie is scared because she's not in control, and she doesn't like the way she's acting. Many little listeners will know exactly how she feels.

The Squeaky Door

By Margaret Read MacDonald. Illustrated by Mary Newell DePalma. HarperCollins, 2006. Ages 4–6.

MacDonald—storyteller, author, and children's librarian—brings her experience to bear in this straightforward retelling of an old favorite, distinguished by the way the words are set down on the page. Ellipses, uppercase letters, exclamation points, and divergent spellings ("squeeeeeak!") signal adult readers to pause, raise or lower their voice, or inject drama into the cumulative tale of a misguided grandma who can't figure out why her grandson can't sleep in a big-boy bed. Finally realizing what's really causing the problem, she finds a quick solution: "She oiled that squeaky door."

Thank You, God, for Everything

By August Gold. Illustrated by Wendy Anderson Halperin. Putnam, 2009. Ages 5–7.

Gold aims to "show young readers how to develop their own thankful eyes." Daisy doesn't know what to be thankful for. Her mother tells her to look around, and when she does, she sees blessings everywhere: the people she meets, the things she's able to do, the places she can go, even those hugs from Grandma. By the close, Daisy knows to thank God for everything.

Thunder-Boomer!

By Shutta Crum. Illustrated by Carol Thompson. Clarion, 2009. Ages 4–6.

A farm family runs for shelter just before a thunderstorm hits. The storm is exciting but worrisome, too, as the children hear the hail and booming thunder and watch lightning streak across the sky. Sound-effect words have been integrated into the pictures, and a secondary story involving the antics of a hen adds a nice bit of humor to what could have been a little scary.

Time for Ballet

By Adele Geras. Illustrated Shelagh McNicholas. Dial, 2004. Ages 4–6.

Warmth shines through this story of young ballet dancers. Preschooler Tilly talks about her ballet class where, along with her classmates, she learns the five basic positions and practices how to walk like a dinosaur and soar like a butterfly. She also describes how she practices at home for her part in an upcoming ballet show; sometimes she's "a leapy cat, a curled-up-to-sleepy cat, a stretchy cat / a pounce-on-a-mousey cat." Details of everyday life and the gangly, sometimes awkward movements of a child learning ballet make identifying with Tilly easy. Follow up with *Little Ballet Star*, in which Tilly sees her beautiful aunt dance onstage. Both stories are sure to resonate with lots of little girls.

Trouble Gum

By Matthew Cordell. Illustrated by the author. Feiwel and Friends, 2009. Ages 4–6.

Bubbles, bubbles, and more bubbles. This book is filled with them, beginning with the cover art, which shows a very, very small pig (Ruben) blowing a very, very big bubble that completely surrounds the title. Ruben is delighted when he receives some gum from his visiting grandmother, and he gets right to work, totally ignoring his mother's bubble-blowing rules. What a mess when a giant bubble bursts—but what fun! If this is a hit, try one of the popular Rotten Ralph books by Jack Gantos. Rotten Ralph, a naughty cat, doesn't like rules either.

A Very Big Bunny

By Marisabina Russo. Illustrated by the author. Schwartz & Wade, 2010. Ages 4–6.

Amelia is tall—much taller than other bunnies her age. Her well-meaning mother doesn't help much when she tells her, "You really stand out in a crowd." Because Amelia's so big, her bunny classmates think she's weird and won't play with her. Susannah, the smallest bunny in Amelia's class, has a similar problem; nobody plays with her either. That the two eventually become friends is a given. While the ending is happy, the book realistically captures what it's like to be labeled as different.

What's Special about Me, Mama?

By Kristina Evans. Illustrated by Javaka Steptoe. Hyperion, 2011. Ages 4–6.

The title question forms the basis of a tender conversation between an African American boy and his mother. The mother has no shortage of comforting things to say. She tells her son he's beautiful and amazing, and that she loves to hear him laugh. But what means the most to the boy is his mother's wonderful hug, which convinces him all his very special parts make up a special whole.

Wemberly Worried

By Kevin Henkes. Illustrated by the author. Greenwillow, 2000. Ages 4–6.

Mouse girl Wemberly worries about everything. Silly things and important things. Will she shrink in the bath? Does the radiator's hiss mean that a snake has crawled inside? She's even been known to visit her parents at night to make sure they are still there. Her doll Petal—her version of a security blanket—rarely leaves her side. Wemberly's first day at New Morning Nursery School is shaping up to be a total nightmare. The teacher is sure to be mean, and Wemberly is certain she won't fit in.

Lucky for Wemberly she finds a classmate, Jewel (who arrives with her own animal friend), who makes everything seem more manageable. For the flip side of worrywart Wemberly, read one of Henkes's books about irrepressible Lilly.

What Happens on Wednesdays

By Emily Jenkins. Illustrated by Laura Castillo. Farrar Strauss Giroux, 2007. Ages 4–6.

The ordinary becomes special in a journey through a young child's full and busy weekday. A little girl describes what she does from waking and spending quality time with Mom to going to school, napping, and after a busy afternoon, finally going to bed. The familiar daily activities will draw listeners right into the story.

When You Are Happy

By Eileen Spinelli. Illustrated by Geraldo Valério. Simon & Schuster, 2006. Ages 4–6.

In a comforting story laced together by the refrain "When you are . . . ," each member of a little girl's family pledges to care for her. Colorful illustrations add a bit of whimsy to the sentiment. When the child is sick, Mom and Dad wait on her; when she is grumpy her brothers and sisters make her laugh; when she is lost her grandfather looks for her in a helicopter; and when she is afraid, there's someone who will "take her hand / and not let go." A warm celebration of family and of unconditional love.

Which Shoes Would You Choose?

By Betsy R. Rosenthal. Illustrated by Nancy Cote. Putnam, 2010. Ages 4–6.

This appealing guessing game challenges children to select the footwear a boy named Sherman will wear during the day. "Which shoes does he choose?" Which shoes are best for a particular activity? "Does Sherman wear skates when he goes out to eat?" The answer pictures show how the footwear should be worn. Little ones following along will have strong opinions about Sherman's choices, and his exceptional array of footwear—from flip-flops and galoshes to roller skates—give them plenty of opportunity to comment.

Who Has What? All about Girls' Bodies and Boys' Bodies

By Robie H. Harris. Illustrated by Nadine Bernard Westcott. Candlewick, 2011. Ages 4–7.

"Every girl has a body. Every boy has a body. Every grown-up has a body." But "who has what?" A family trip to the beach provides opportunity for parents to answer the question. While they explain, small arrows in the pictures indicate each body part. After pointing out the many parts that are the same in the children, they tackle the differences in straightforward, very simple terms—for example "[Girls] have an opening to the vagina, [and] an opening where pee comes out." Westcott's cheerful artwork keeps the tone light. The explanations will probably be enough to satisfy the curiosity of most four- to seven-year-olds, but prepare for questions anyway.

Yoko's Show-and-Tell

By Rosemary Wells. Illustrated by the author. Hyperion, 2011. Ages 4–6.

Yoko, a Japanese kitty stand-in for a child, receives an antique doll named Miki. She wants to take Miki to school for show-and-tell to help her explain about a traditional Japanese holiday and doll festival. Her mother says no, but Yoko takes Miki anyway, and the doll is accidentally broken. A sorrowful Yoko confesses and takes responsibility. Mom is disappointed and angry, but by taking the toy to the doll hospital, she reassures her child that she is still loved. When the toy comes home, it looks good as new. In *Yoko Learns to Read*, the mother and daughter draw closer as they both learn to read English.

Zero

By Kathryn Otoshi. Illustrated by the author. KO Kids, 2010. Ages 4–7.

On one level, this clever book is about numbers; on another it's about self-worth. Zero thinks her name fits her perfectly. She feels plain, unexciting, and empty inside. She just doesn't count. Twisting herself into a 1, an 8 or a 9 turns out to be uncomfortable and silly. Wise number 7 tells her that everybody counts: "Be open. You'll find a way." Taking the advice to heart, she hooks herself to other numerals to make 10, 20, 100, raising not only her own self-esteem but paving the way for others to do the same. Just as successful is Otoshi's *One*, which introduces the topic of bullying.

4

FAMILY

Biological, nuclear, extended, blended, crosscultural, single parent—no matter how you define family, it plays an integral part in readying a child for life. It's a safe haven, a comfort zone, and a preschool all rolled into one. No wonder family, parent-child, and sibling relationships are frequent topics for children's book authors. The titles in this section model strong, nurturing, joyful connections, even in the face of the confusions, anxieties, jealousies, wacky situations, and disappointments that are a natural part of family life.

And Tango Makes Three
By Justin Richardson and Peter Parnell. Illustrated by Henry Cole.
Simon & Schuster, 2005. Ages 5–8.

This straightforward book, based on a true story about two penguins in New York City's Central Park Zoo, works on two levels. Young children will enjoy it as a pleasant glimpse of a penguin family at a busy zoo. For older ones, it can serve to open discussion about different family structures. Two male chinstrap penguins, Roy and Silo, share a nest like other penguin couples. When other pairs start hatching eggs, they bring a rock to their nest and proceed to care for it. Deciding the pair should have a chance to be parents, a discerning zookeeper gives them a real egg, which the penguin papas care for, just like other penguin pairs. The egg eventually hatches into a baby daughter, Tango, and her penguin fathers "knew just what to do."

Angelina's Island

By Jeanette Winter. Illustrated by the author. Farrar Straus Giroux, 2007. Ages 4–6.

Newly arrived in New York, Angelina misses everything about her native Jamaica: the food, the weather, the games she played with her friends. Her new country is different and hard to get used to. Then her mother discovers that Carnival, one of the biggest events on the Jamaican calendar, is celebrated in Brooklyn, and arranges to have a beautiful costume made for Angelina so that she can participate. Many listeners can relate to Angelina's confusion and anxiety at being in a new and strange place—and also her joy at finding a link to her old home.

Apple Pie Fourth of July

By Janet S. Wong. Illustrated by Margaret Chodos-Irvine. Harcourt, 2002. Ages 4–6.

"My parents do not understand all American things. They were not born here," complains a young Chinese American girl who is missing the Fourth of July parade to work in her parents' food store. She's convinced that nobody wants chow mein on this day; they want hot dogs, potato salad, and above all, apple pie. To her surprise, when the parades are done, neighbors pour into the store; everyone is now hungry for Chinese takeout. Later, after the rush has subsided and the store has closed, the girl and her loving parents do "American things": they watch fireworks and eat apple pie.

Big Brothers Don't Take Naps

By Louise Borden. Illustrated by Emma Dodd. Margaret K. McElderry, 2011. Ages 4–6.

Nicholas thinks his big brother is terrific. James can write his name, make up great games, read long books, and go to school by himself on the bus. Even more awesome is the fact that James never has to stop having fun to take a nap. Nick longs to be just like James. When the boys' new sister is born, Nick gets his wish. Now he's a big brother himself, which, of course, means *no more naps.*

Big Red Lollipop

By Rukhsana Khan. Illustrated by Sophie Blackall. Viking, 2010. Ages 4–7.

When Rubina, living in America, is invited to a birthday party, her Pakistani mother—who, unlike her daughters, still wears traditional garb—insists she take along middle sister Sana. If that weren't bad enough, Sana eats the lollipop that Rubina has saved from her goodie bag. When Sana receives her own birthday invitation, Mother decrees littlest sister

Maryam should go, too. At first Rubina is glad Sana will suffer the same embarrassment she did. But as she remembers how bad she felt, she puts her resentment aside and convinces their mother that adapting to new ways isn't a bad thing. In a sweet finale, Sana gives Rubina a new lollipop, a symbol of both her gratitude and her contrition.

Blackout
By John Rocco. Illustrated by the author. Hyperion, 2011. Ages 4–6.

A break in the normal routine can be scary for young children, but it can also be a wonderful opportunity to have fun. Rocco's tale of a busy urban family during a blackout begins with homey scenes: Mom at the computer; Dad in the kitchen; the children doing favorite things in brightly lit surroundings. Suddenly the lights go out, and the family members, drawn together at first by necessity, learn that darkness has a special magic of its own.

Circle Unbroken
By Margot Theis Raven. Illustrated by E. B. Lewis. Farrar Straus Giroux, 2004. Ages 4–7.

In this story, a small woven basket links a modern-day child to her West African roots. Grandmother teaches her granddaughter how to make a sweetgrass basket, a craft brought from Africa to South Carolina and Georgia. She explains how the child's ancestor once harvested tall grasses and wove them into baskets. When he came to this country as a slave, he found similar grasses and continued to weave baskets. He taught others who, as history unfolded around them, passed on their craft, just as Grandmother is doing now. The beautiful words echo the push and pull of the weaving and the enduring connections of family. A historical note about the baskets and a bibliography are appended.

Creaky Old House: A Topsy-Turvy Tale of a Real Fixer-Upper
By Linda Ashman. Illustrated by Michael Chesworth. Sterling, 2009. Ages 4–6.

The chaos of a large family working and playing in an old house comes to a halt when the doorknob falls off the front door. It "looks like it needs a screw." It's soon clear, however, that a screw won't do. Neither will a new knob or a new door. Perhaps a new house is the best way to go. When the frenzied family finally takes a breather from suggesting increasingly complicated fixes, it discovers that toddler Lizzie has solved the problem—in the simplest way imaginable. For another whimsical book about a baby in the know, try *Edwin Speaks Up*, by April Stevens.

Daddy Goes to Work

By Jabari Asim. Illustrated by Aaron Boyd. Little, Brown, 2006. Ages 4–6.

There are lots of books about dads and daughters but few about Dads taking daughters to work—and fewer still with African American characters. In this one, a little girl begins her day with Dad on the commuter train. When they arrive in the big city, they go to the tall building where Dad works and ride the elevator up to his office. After lunch in the park, it's back to work, the return trip home, and a sweet goodnight scene to mark the end of a perfect day. The warmth between the child and the parent is evident on every page of this unpretentious slice of life.

A Drive in the Country

By Michael J. Rosen. Illustrated by Marc Burckhardt. Candlewick, 2007. Ages 4–6.

Although trips in the country with the kids have strong competition from soccer and baseball and even computers, this idyllic scenario gives the idea a boost. After loading the car with a variety of games and snacks (and, of course, the dog), a family heads down the road to see what there is to see. They play silly games, sing songs, smell country smells (stinky and sweet), and wade in a lake, imparting a charming vision of togetherness.

Every Friday

By Dan Yaccarino. Illustrated by the author. Holt, 2007. Ages 4–6.

"Friday is my favorite day," declares a young city boy, who proceeds to describe his Friday breakfast outing with Dad. On their way to the diner, they mail a letter, greet people they know, and see how the street scene has changed from the previous week. Over pancakes they talk about "all sorts of things" as a busy waitress serves coffee and people read their morning papers. The artwork suggests the story takes place in a time gone by: milk bottles stand outside the apartment door; Dad wears a suit and fedora. But no matter the backdrop, what comes clear is how much each half of the pair enjoys their special time together.

Grandma Calls Me Beautiful

By Barbara M. Joosse. Illustrated by Barbara Lavallee. Chronicle, 2008. Ages 4–6.

Set in Hawai'i, this tender story depicts a devoted relationship between a grandmother and her grandchild. A young girl begs to her grandmother to tell "our story." Grandma obliges, recalling a baby "bright as a kukui torch" whom Grandma calls Beautiful and who grows into the lovely child. A scattering of Hawaiian terms and cultural elements, and art-work in vibrant colors, convey a vivid sense of place.

The Great Big Book of Families

By Mary Hoffman. Illustrated by Ros Asquith. Dial, 2010. Ages 4–7.

Be prepared for your child to spend lots of private time looking at the cartoon artwork in this tribute to family. Pictures gather together all kinds of families: black, white, brown, interracial; nuclear and extended families, families with same-sex parents, foster, adoptive and single-parent families. They work, play, eat, argue. They experience hard times and celebrate joyful occasions. The differences among the families are striking, but so are the similarities. Each picture is an opportunity for a child to fill in a family's story.

Guji Guji

By Chih-Yuan Chen. Illustrated by the author. Kane/Miller, 2004. Ages 4–6.

A surprise awaits Mama Duck when her eggs hatch. Out pops a crocodile! Despite his lack of feathers, the little guy is accepted as part of the family. Sneers from other crocs, however, bring home the truth about his difference and force him to decide which family he belongs to. Guess which one he chooses. Many countries have a version of the ugly duckling story; this one, published in Taiwan, is both charmingly told and humorously illustrated. Cheryl Bardoe's *The Ugly Duckling Dinosaur: A Prehistoric Tale*, which ends quite differently, is another version worth sharing.

The Hello, Goodbye Window

By Norton Juster. Illustrated by Chris Raschka. Michael Di Capua, 2005. Ages 4–6.

Nanna and Poppy love having their granddaughter spend the day, and the child loves being with them. The little girl rides her bike, watches as her grandparents go about their various activities, and takes a nap—all the while feeling safe and loved in the real world of her interracial family. Her imagination takes over as she looks out her grandparents' kitchen window, which Nanna insists is magic. From there she sees all manner of wonderful things: a striped cat becomes a tiger; the Queen of England arrives for tea. She also sees her loving parents arriving to pick her up at the end of the day. The playful artwork—all swirls and squiggles and patches of paint—purposefully calls to mind a child's own simple coloring. Nanna, Poppy, and their granddaughter appear together again in *Sourpuss and Sweetie Pie*, about the little girl's ever-changing moods.

Henry's First-Moon Birthday

By Lenore Look. Illustrated by Yumi Heo. Atheneum, 2001. Ages 4–6.

Jenny has always helped care for her baby brother, Henry. To celebrate his first birthday in the traditional Chinese fashion, the family plans a first-moon birthday party. While she works alongside Gnin Gnin, her grandmother, she chats about the goings-on: special good luck messages, the food, her new dress, doting relatives. Her pique at Henry for getting all the attention is only temporary—and utterly realistic. By the end of the day, there's no doubt about her love. Family chaos, sibling rivalry, and a glimpse of Chinese culture are rolled into a tidy, very pleasing package.

How to Be a Baby . . . by Me, the Big Sister

By Sally Lloyd-Jones. Illustrated by Sue Heap. Schwartz and Wade, 2007. Ages 4–6.

A sassy child narrator offers a clever, comical take on sibling rivalry. She sets herself squarely apart from babies in general by informing them (especially her little brother, who looks on) just what they can't do. Along with being exceptionally sure of herself, she knows her baby stuff. "When you're a baby you can't . . ." dress yourself, dance, go to school, or have friends. When you talk, nobody understands you, and you can't even appreciate TV! But after getting all that out into the open, she also lists some good things about being a baby (nothing is your fault), and she even admits she might occasionally enjoy having someone adore her like they coo over her brother. Older sibs will delight in seeing some of their own opinions expressed so perfectly by someone else.

I Love Saturdays y domingos

By Alma Flor Ada. Illustrated by Elivia Savadier. Atheneum, 2002. Ages 4–6.

On Saturdays a little girl visits Grandma and Grandpa; she spends Sundays, *los domingos*, with *abuelito y abuelita*, her Mexican American grandparents. She's obviously cherished by all four, and she moves easily between the two cultures and the variety of things she does during her weekends. Spanish terms, easily understood in context, are scattered throughout a story that celebrates a child's dual heritage.

Henry's First-Moon Birthday by Lenore Look

Little Mamá Forgets

By Robin Cruise. Illustrated by Stacey Dressen-McQueen. Farrar Straus Giroux, 2006. Ages 4–6.

Lucy's aging grandmother is losing her memory. Little Mamá does recall some things. She still brushes Lucy's hair each night, a perfect one hundred strokes, but other things, like how to clean her teeth, are lost to her until Lucy explains how to do them. Regardless of the changes Lucy sees in her beloved relative, she has a scrapbook full of pictures to share with her grandmother and an abiding affection for the woman, who is dearly loved by her whole Mexican American family. Vibrant, colorful artwork reflects the story's cultural backdrop, at the same time helping to make the realism at the heart of the story easier for young children to handle.

Mamá and Me

By Arthur Dorros. Illustrated by Rudy Gutierrez. Rayo. 2011. Ages 4–6.

Like Dorros's previous book *Papá and Me,* this story celebrates a parent-child bond during what seems to be an ordinary day. A mother and daughter fill their time together with pleasant activities: they visit family, bake cookies, shop. But all the while the little girl has a secret; she has been preparing a big surprise party for her mother, to which the whole family is invited. *"¡Feliz día de las madres!"* A festive book to share on Mom's birthday.

Mama's Saris

By Pooja Makhijani. Illustrated by Elena Gomez. Little, Brown, 2007. Ages 4–6.

Watching as her mother puts on one of her lovely saris, an East Indian child living in America admires its beauty, so different from the slacks and sweaters her mother wears to work. Now that she is growing up, she longs to wear one, too. Together mother and daughter recall the occasions when Mama wore each of her saris. The to the girl's delight, Mama drapes her lovingly in a wrap of vivid blue. The Hindi phrases are clearly defined in an introductory glossary. Pair this with Sandhya Rao's *My Mother's Sari*.

Many Ways: How Families Practice Their Beliefs and Religions

By Shelley Rotner and Sheila M. Kelly. Illustrated with photographs by Shelley Rotner. Millbrook, 2006. Ages: 4–7.

With references to religion so often in the news, it's natural for children to ask questions. Rotner's photo essay sets out to answer some of them by introducing six different faiths: Buddhism, Christianity, Hinduism, Islam, Judaism, and Sikhism. The text provides plenty of information while keeping the age level of the audience clearly in mind, and clear, colorful photographs show places of worship, religious symbols, distinctive practices, and children and adults worshiping—together and as individuals.

Molly and Her Dad

By Jan Ormerod. Illustrated by Carol Thompson. Roaring Brook, 2008. Ages 4–6.

Claire Masurel's *Two Homes* (below) depicts a child shuttling between the homes of two loving parents. In this book, a young girl, Molly, barely knows her father, who lives very far away. Molly loves to make up stories about him: he's a famous artist, an astronaut, an explorer. Then Molly's mom has to take a trip, and her father, who is big and loud and silly, comes to stay. She's wary of him at first. She doesn't even know what to call him. Daddy? Joe? What's more, he's not at all what she imagined. But as "Papa" wins over her friends with his humor and great stories, Molly begins to appreciate him as he really is. Bo R. Holmberg also writes

followed by a string of ideas for ridding themselves of the noisy, bald-headed intruder. The cartoonlike pictures moderate the irony, keeping the tone appropriately lighthearted as the dogs come to appreciate the weird-smelling new addition to the household.

Trudy
By Henry Cole. Illustrated by the author. Greenwillow, 2009. Ages 4–6.

Esme, who lives on a farm with her grandparents, wants a pet—"not too big . . . not too small, and not stinky." Her grandfather finds the perfect one at the county auction: Trudy the goat. It soon becomes apparent that Trudy is special in a peculiar way. Every time she moves into the barn, it snows. News of her talent spreads; she becomes a media celebrity. One day, however, she moves into the barn and snowflakes don't fly. Nor does her exit from the barn herald a change in the weather. What follows Trudy from the barn is her new baby goat, which apparently has inherited a forecasting talent all its own.

The Twins' Blanket
By Hyewon Yum. Illustrated by the author. Farrar Strauss Giroux, 2011. Ages 4–6.

What's it like to be a twin? In alternating voices twin girls talk about their likes, dislikes, and affection for each other. Having shared everything since infancy, the girls are now ready to move into twin beds. But which girl will take the beloved blanket that covers their old bed? Mom comes up with a solution: each child is given half the blanket, which Mom sews onto new coverlets—one pink and one yellow. The different colors mark the girl's first steps toward independence; the old blanket marks their forever connection.

Two Homes
By Claire Masurel. Illustrated by Kady MacDonald Denton. Candlewick, 2001. Ages 4–6.

Alex has two homes. Sometimes he lives at his dad's house; at other times he lives with Mommy in her apartment in the city. He also has two bedrooms, two toothbrushes. He loves both his parents equally and loves to be with them. Each picture spread shows the boy engaged in similar activities at his different homes. The ending affirms Alex is loved no matter where he is, and no matter where his parents are. Nancy Coffelt's *Fred Stays with Me!*—in which a child's bond with her dog helps her handle her parents' divorce—delves more deeply into the emotional upheaval that sometimes comes with living in two places.

Tyrannosaurus Dad

By Liz Rosenberg. Illustrated by Matthew Myers. Roaring Brook, 2011. Ages 5–7.

Like other dads whose children go to Elmwood Elementary School, Tobias's father mows the lawn, likes to barbecue, has a favorite chair, and goes to work each day. Unlike other children's dads, Tobias's pop has very sharp teeth, a long tail, and happens to be green. That nobody much notices the difference between dinosaur Dad and human son is part of the fun of a book that can double as a lesson in blended families.

Uncle Peter's Amazing Chinese Wedding

By Lenore Look. Illustrated by Yumi Heo. Atheneum, 2006. Ages 4–6.

Chinese American Jenny, introduced in *Henry's First-Moon Birthday*, adores Uncle Peter, who has always given her lots of attention. When his wedding rolls around, however, his attention is elsewhere. Jenny feels slighted, like "an umbrella turned inside out." Her anger bubbles out in a silly stunt, and then fizzles as she becomes involved in the many Chinese wedding traditions. A relationship with Uncle Peter's new wife is cemented when Stella chooses Jenny for a very special wedding task. Pair this with Kevin Henkes's *Lilly's Big Day*, about a feisty little mouse who convinces herself she's going to be the flower girl in her teacher's wedding.

Underground

By Shane W. Evans. Illustrated by the author. Neal Porter, 2011. Ages 5–7.

The title refers to the Underground Railroad, a way out of slavery for the family in this picture book. Words are few, perhaps four or five to a page; yet listeners still experience the gripping emotion of the escape. A courageous but frightened family leaves quietly, cloaked in darkness. They run, and then crawl. They travel by wagon, pursued by slave catchers and helped by friends. When they reach their destination, a rising sun welcomes them and helps them celebrate the birth of a new child, the first born free. Try this as a family read-aloud. Preschoolers will respond to the drama; older children will ask for more history.

What Will You Be, Sara Mee?

By Kate Aver Avraham. Illustrated by Anne Sibley O'Brien. Charlesbridge, 2010. Ages 4–6.

First birthday festivals are traditional in many cultures (see *Henry's First-Moon Birthday*). This birthday tale is narrated by the birthday girl's elder brother, Chong. Chong explains the Korean celebration of *tol* to his baby sister, telling her he's particularly looking forward to *toljabee*, a game in which the birthday child chooses an object that tradition dictates will serve as a clue to her future. What will you be, Sara Mee? A glossary of the Korean words scattered through the story, along with an author's note at the end, offer more information for parents to share.

Would I Trade My Parents?
By Laura Numeroff. Illustrated by James Bernardin. Abrams, 2009. Ages 5–7.

What kid hasn't thought about trading in his or her parents for new ones? When an observant young boy visits the houses of his friends, the thought crosses his mind. Other parents have interesting jobs; the boy's dad is writer, and his mother teaches French. Other parents don't care what their kids eat and allow pets; not his. But his mother tells good jokes, his dad knows all about nature, and they both take time to read him stories. That makes him think they love him, which helps him decide he's got pretty good parents after all: "I wouldn't trade my parents. I know they're the best."

5

FRIENDSHIP

D o friends always agree? Can a friend make you mad? How long does friendship last? Can you have more than one best friend? Can your dog be your friend? What about somebody who isn't real? The books below capture the wonder, the closeness, the anger, and the jealousy of friendship. Their child characters (and animal surrogates) star in stories that can spur little listeners to think about what friendship means to them.

Alex and Lulu: Two of a Kind

By Lorena Siminovich. Illustrated by the author. Candlewick, 2009. Ages 4–6.

Alex and Lulu like to run, jump, and swing on the swings. That's part of what makes them friends. But they do have differences, the most obvious being that Alex is a dog and Lulu is a cat. Alex likes soccer; Lulu would rather paint pictures. Given their dissimilar interests, Alex begins to wonder if they really are friends after all. Lulu convinces him otherwise—after all, they both like pillow fights, and they very much like spending time together. Built into the honest friendship story is a clever mini-lesson in true opposites, such as *big/small, wet/dry.*

The Bear Who Shared

By Catherine Rayner. Illustrated by the author. Dial, 2011. Ages 4–6.

Norris the bear is camped out beneath a tree, waiting impatiently for its luscious fruit to drop: "It smelled of honey and sunny days." Meanwhile

Tulip and Violet (a raccoon and a mouse) are just as eager to get at the fruit. When the fruit finally falls, plopping right on Norris's head, he recognizes there's plenty for all and shares it, making two fast friends.

Best Best Friends

By Margaret Chodos-Irvine. Illustrated by the author. Harcourt, 2006. Ages 4–6.

Friends one day, but not the next? Preschoolers Clare and Mary do everything together; they even hold hands on the playground. Then Mary's birthday rolls around, with cupcakes and a crown to mark the occasion. Jealous and angry at Mary for getting so much attention, Clare starts an argument, which culminates in both girls furiously declaring, "YOU ARE NOT MY FRIEND!" Later, when time apart has worked a bit of magic, Clare feels ashamed of herself. She draws Mary a birthday picture, which her friend gracefully accepts as an apology. The author gets the give-and-take of true friendship exactly right.

City Dog, Country Frog

By Mo Willems. Illustrated by Jon J. Muth. Hyperion, 2010. Ages 4–6.

It's spring vacation for City Dog, who is delighted to have a chance to investigate new territory. While exploring, he comes upon a green frog, who tells Dog that he's waiting for a friend: "But you'll do." During the spring and throughout the summer, the pair finds myriad things to do. When Dog returns in the fall, Frog is too tired to play, so he and Dog reminisce about the good times they had in the past. In winter, Frog is nowhere to be found; nor is he around when Dog comes back the following spring. One day when Dog is missing his old friend, a chipmunk comes by. "What are you doing?" she asks. Reminded of Frog, Dog tells her he's waiting for a friend: "But you'll do." The march of the seasons is a reassuring backdrop to this simply written but layered story about friendship and loss.

Dog and Bear: Two Friends, Three Stories

By Laura Vaccaro Seeger. Illustrated by the author. Neal Porter, 2012. Ages 4–5.

Bear is a stuffed toy, and Dog is an energetic dachshund. It's a pretty odd friendship, but it survives quite well despite the ups and downs depicted in the three short episodes gathered together in this tidy volume. In the first story Dog helps his fearful friend down from a chair so the two can go outdoors. In the second, Bear gently explains to his pal that he would rather finish his book than play. And in the third, Bear counsels Dog about a name change. The endearing partnership is extended in two more books—*Dog and Bear: Two's Company* and *Dog and Bear: Three to Get Ready.* All three make good read-alouds, but their short story format also makes them ideal for children just stepping into chapter books.

The Dog Who Belonged to No One
By Amy Hest. Illustrated by Amy Bates. Abrams, 2008. Ages 4–6.

Children and cute dogs are partnered in many picture books. The pairing in this old-fashioned story is particularly endearing. A vagabond brown-and-white pup travels through a town in search of a friend and a home. Meanwhile, a little girl on a bike delivers food to her parents' customers, making up stories to offset the loneliness of her ride. One stormy day the two meet. The dog dashes through the rain alongside the little girl, who pedals furiously to her house, where a warm welcome awaits them both. *Before You Were Mine*, by Maribeth Boelts, is another winning child-dog story. In this tale, a little boy speculates about what life might have been like for the shelter dog that has come to live with his family.

A Friend
By Anette Bley. Illustrated by the author. Kane/Miller, 2009. Ages 4–5.

Although this book was first published in Germany, the feelings and friendships it depicts are universal. There's no story in the traditional sense. Rather, the content comprises a series of pictures about many different people in many different situations, each of which contributes in some way to a young child's understanding of what friendship is. Could it be a little boy taking comfort from a grown-up? Or is it a child whispering secrets into a playmate's ear? Children can imagine their own stories to fit the art and then share them with the person sitting beside them.

Half a World Away
By Libby Gleeson. Illustrated by Freya Blackwood. Scholastic, 2007. Ages 4–7.

When Amy's family moves to a big city across the ocean, Louie misses her terribly. He knows when he's awake, she will be sleeping, and he wonders what her new home is like. Will she still build towers and play adventure games? Does she miss him as much as he misses her? Most of all he wonders if she will hear him if he yells their special word, "Cooo-ee! Cooo-ee!" Grandma tells him anything is possible, so Louie gives it a try. When Amy wakes the next day, she has dreamt about her good friend calling "Cooo-ee" from "half a world away." Tender, honest, and sweetly magical, this is one of the few stories about friends of different genders.

Horace and Morris Say Cheese
(Which Makes Dolores Sneeze!)

By James Howe. Illustrated by Amy Walrod. Atheneum, 2009. Ages 4–6.

Dolores the mouse is allergic to cheese, and because she can't eat it, she can think of nothing else. Swiss cheese, cheese and crackers, cheese curls, cheese fondue—visions of cheese float around her head. To make things worse, Muenster Movie Madness is at the local theater, which is right next door to the Fromage Garage. For someone less determined, "The Everything Cheese Festival" might have been the last straw, but clever Dolores finds a way to have a cheese-free great time with her two best friends. Food allergies are tough for many kids to handle; the "cheesy" humor of Dolores's dilemma provides a bit of fun while acknowledging a real problem.

Hurry Up and Slow Down

By Layn Marlow. Illustrated by the author. Holiday, 2009. Ages 4–6.

Marlow turns a classic tale of rivalry into a friendship story. "Hare is always in a hurry"; his pal tortoise, shown much smaller and farther away in the pictures, is not. That's old news. But when Tortoise reads Hare a bedtime story, the impatient rabbit begs his friend to slow down! He wants to have more time to look at the pictures. The contrast between the buddies comes through not only in the pictures but also in the way the words appear on the page. Energetic Hare's comments to his slow companion appear in a large, playful font, while descriptions of Tortoise plugging along are set down in a slow, steady rhythm. The resulting "dialogue" between the two pals will enrich the read-aloud experience.

I Repeat, Don't Cheat!

By Margery Cuyler. Illustrated by Arthur Howard. Simon & Schuster, 2010. Ages 4–6.

Jessica's friend Lizzie has a problem. She cheats. She copies Jessica's work in school; she cheats at games; she even tells outright lies. It makes Jessica angry, especially when Lizzie takes credit for something Jessica really did. Jessica's not sure what to do. Isn't she abetting her friend's dishonesty by keeping quiet? Then again, the girls do everything together. Shouldn't loyalty to her friend come first? Jessica finally does the right thing—and Lizzie does, too. The happy ending is pretty simplistic, but the book offers a terrific opportunity to begin a conversation about a situation children frequently encounter among friends and even within families.

Imagine Harry

By Kate Klise. Illustrated by M. Sarah Klise. Harcourt, 2007. Ages 4–6.

Little Rabbit has an invisible friend called Harry. They play together, and Mother Rabbit makes sure that Harry is included when she passes out snacks. Things change, though, when Little Rabbit starts school. One day while Little Rabbit is enjoying an activity, Harry goes off to take a nap. After school, when Mother politely asks after Harry, Little Rabbit surprises them both by telling her that Harry has moved away. A gentle story about the importance and transience of imaginary friends.

Moon Rabbit

By Natalie Russell. Illustrated by the author. Viking, 2009. Ages 4–6.

One evening, as a patchwork moon shines bright, pensive Little Rabbit hears lovely music coming from deep in the forest. Leaving the city behind, she follows the sound and comes upon Brown Rabbit playing his guitar. The music lightens Little Rabbit's heart, and she begins to dance. Later the rabbits trade stories and become friends. But Little Rabbit misses the hustle and bustle of home. She knows Brown Rabbit's life is not for her, and the two friends part with promises to meet again. The story continues in *Brown Rabbit in the City*. Follow up with Jan Brett's *Town Mouse, Country Mouse*.

Mr. Duck Means Business

By Tammi Sauer. Illustrated by Jeff Mack. Paula Wiseman, 2011. Ages 4–6.

Mr. Duck arrives at the pond for his morning swim at precisely 8:01. He glides along, confident that his carefully painted "No Visitors Welcome" sign will keep intruders away. No such luck. One very hot day, his peace is shattered by a bevy of barnyard animals jumping joyously into the cool water. Mr. Duck is enraged. How could they disturb his peace? Quacking and flapping for all he's worth, he chases the noisy interlopers away, only to decide that it's now much too quiet for his liking. He picks up his paintbrush and amends his sign. Leaving himself space for quiet contemplation, he invites others to join him every day at 2:00.

My Friend Jamal

By Anna McQuinn. Photography by the author. Artwork by Ben Frey. Annick, 2008. Ages 4–6.

Joseph and Jamal, both born in Canada, are classmates and friends, but their family stories are quite different. Jamal's Muslim parents fled war-torn Somalia, leaving behind relatives whom Jamal has never met. Joseph's family emigrated from Poland: his grandmother came, too. Jamal's mother, who already knows several languages, is learning English and how to use the computer. Joseph's mother helps him do homework. Other differences between the families appear in the artwork, a combination of photos and painted details, which also show what the boys have most in common—a friendship that respects difference.

My Friend Rabbit

By Eric Rohmann. Illustrated by the author. Roaring Brook, 2002. Ages 4–6.

Mouse's friend Rabbit has good intentions, but he's always causing trouble. How much trouble? Mouse gives an example. Take the time Rabbit hurled Mouse's biplane into the branches of a tree. Realizing his mistake, Rabbit promises a solution. Beginning with an elephant, Rabbit drags a motley crew of animals into view. One atop the other, they form an animal pyramid, with Mouse at the top. Just as Mouse retrieves his beloved plane the pyramid tumbles, releasing a perturbed bunch of beasts, all anxious to lay their claws, paws, and webbed feet on Rabbit. Mouse, now safely in his plane, comes to the rescue of his well-meaning friend. The slapstick humor is terrific, as is the glorious animal pyramid, which readers can see in full by turning the book vertically. This also available as a board book.

Neville

By Norton Juster. Illustrated by G. Brian Karas. Schwartz & Wade, 2011. Ages 4–7.

After a long car trip, a boy and his family arrive at their new home. The child realizes everything will be different, but he worries most about being lonely. Will he be able to find new friends? The test comes when his mother sends him outdoors. As he takes a tour of his new block, he calls out, "NEVILLE, NEVILLE." It isn't long before kids turn out to help him find the mysterious Neville, whom the boy describes in some detail. The neighborhood kids can't wait to make friends with the mystery boy, whose identity is finally revealed at the end of the story. Some listeners are sure to guess; many will be delightfully surprised.

Poindexter Makes a Friend

By Mike Twohy. Illustrated by the author. Paula Wiseman, 2011. Ages 4–6.

Poindexter, a bashful young pig who works at the library, helps an equally shy turtle, Shelby, find a book on how to make friends. The two read it together and discuss the advice. When they have finished, they select a new book and, now fast friends, go to Pointdexter's house to do some more reading. Other books that touch on shyness and friendship include Daniel Kirk's *Library Mouse: A Friend's Tale*, in which a boy coaxes a timid mouse out of hiding to write a book, and Jacqui Robbins's *The New Girl . . . and Me*, about a shy child who takes a new classmate under her wing.

Pouch!

By David Ezra Stein. Illustrated by the author. Putnam, 2009. Ages 4–6.

Joey the kangaroo is anxious to get out of his mother's pouch and see the world. But he's not quite ready to handle what's out there. His first peek outside puts him face to face with a bee. "Pouch," he cries to Mama as he hurries back to safety. On his next outing he encounters a rabbit. Back inside the pouch he goes. When he spots another baby kangaroo, he's ready to run again—until he realizes the other baby is as uncertain about the world "outside" as he is; perhaps, as friends, they can face it together. Twin themes—little one's tentative steps toward independence and the value of friendship—make this doubly appealing.

Rabbit's Gift

By George Shannon. Illustrated by Laura Dronzek. Harcourt, 2007. Ages 4–6.

A rabbit finds two turnips. Because he needs only one for himself, he leaves the other on his friend Donkey's doorstep. Donkey, who has a potato, leaves the turnip for Goat, who leaves it for Deer. Deer, who is happy with her carrot, leaves the turnip for Rabbit. And Rabbit, finding himself in possession of the turnip once again, decides the best thing to do is share it with his three best friends.

Roasted Peanuts

By Tim Egan. Illustrated by the author. Houghton Mifflin, 2006. Ages 4–6.

Sam and Jackson love baseball, and both hope to make the team. Sam, a horse, is agile and strong; he can catch and field and throw. Jackson, a cat, can throw, but he's all thumbs when it comes to catching. It's no surprise when Sam makes the team but Jackson doesn't. Jackson's disappointment doesn't get him down, though. He stays near his good friend and true to baseball and his talent by becoming a peanut vendor, known all over the park for his accurate long-distance tosses.

Scaredy Squirrel Makes a Friend

By Mélanie Watt. Illustrated by the author. Kids Can, 2007. Ages 4–6.

Worrywart Scaredy Squirrel is lonely, but he's too afraid of what can go wrong if he leaves the safety of his tree to look for a friend. After all, bunnies are hopping about on the ground, and maybe they bite. In the pond across the park he spots a goldfish. Perfect. He maps out a careful plan, puts on his name tag, grabs his Scaredy Risk Test, and sets off. What he doesn't count on is a rowdy dog, who, despite first impressions (and teeth), turns out to be a great companion. Like Scaredy's other adventures into the wider world, this one is laugh-out-loud funny. Look for him testing the water in *Scaredy Squirrel at the Beach* and venturing out after dark in *Scaredy Squirrel at Night.*

A Sick Day for Amos McGee

By Philip C. Stead. Illustrated by Erin E. Stead. Neal Porter, 2010. Ages 4–6.

Amos McGee loves his job as zookeeper at a city zoo. He's especially fond of the elephant, the tortoise, the owl, the rhino, and the penguin. He does his best to visit each one every day. One day, he wakes up with a cold and stays home. No chess games with the elephant; no stories for the owl; and no visits to his other animal friends. Imagine his surprise when Elephant, Tortoise, Owl, Rhino, and Penguin show up at his doorstep, ready to cheer him up and care for him in the same way he always cares for them.

A Splendid Friend, Indeed

By Suzanne Bloom. Illustrated by the author. Boyds Mills, 2005. Ages 4–6.

Polar Bear is reading when Goose comes in, takes away his book, and begins reading himself. Later Goose interrupts Bear's writing, then pens his own note. Goose even interrupts Bear's thinking by peppering him with questions. Polar Bear is fed up. But when he sees the note Goose has written, which calls him "splendid friend," he realizes that Goose may be a pest at times, but he's pretty special, too. Goose and Bear return in Bloom's equally charming *Treasure*, and in *What about Bear*, in which Bear suddenly finds himself the odd bear out when Little Fox shows up.

Three by the Sea

By Mini Grey. Illustrated by the author. Knopf, 2011. Ages 4–6.

Dog, Cat, and Mouse live a perfectly happy life in a house by the sea. Dog tends the garden, Mouse cooks, and Cat cleans the place. Enter Fox,

Waddles by David McPhail

representing the Winds of Change Trading Company. He sows the seeds of discontent among the trio, causing them to scrutinize their relationship. Why does Mouse insist on preparing fondue? Why is the garden full of bones? Why does Cat take so many naps? If sly Mr. Fox has a reprehensible outcome in mind, he goes away disappointed. After a near calamity, the three friends work through their discontent, which ultimately strengthens their relationship.

Tiny and Hercules

By Amy Schwartz. Illustrated by the author. Neal Porter, 2009. Ages 4–6.

Best buddies Tiny the elephant and Hercules the mouse star in five stories that explore how two very different friends help each other. In one story Hercules helps slipping, sliding Tiny at the ice rink; in another Tiny helps Hercules' elderly uncle blow out his birthday candles. Pictures add to the gentle humor of the odd couple as they cope with whatever comes their way.

Waddles

By David McPhail. Illustrated by the author. Abrams, 2011. Ages 4–6.

Four short episodes focus on the ups and downs of two animal friends: Waddles the raccoon and Emily the duck. The two have fun together in summer. In spring when Emily needs a break from sitting on her eggs, Waddles volunteers. He scares off a fox just in time to see the ducklings hatch. Emily and her ducklings fly south in the fall, leaving Waddles to spend winter on his own. In spring, when the flock returns to the pond, there's a joyful reunion. A tender story about a friendship that lasts over time.

When Randolph Turned Rotten
By Charise Mericle Harper. Illustrated by the author. Knopf, 2007. Ages 4–6.

Randolph, a beaver, and Ivy, a goose, are great friends—until Ivy is invited to a sleepover birthday party . . . and Randolph isn't. Ivy is going to have a great time, while Randolph is all alone. Jealous and angry, Randolph tries to sabotage the trip. When Ivy goes anyway, Randolph feels terrible; he has hurt his friend's feelings. Will she ever forgive him for being rotten?

You're Mean, Lily Jean!
By Frieda Wishinsky. Illustrated by Kady MacDonald Denton. Albert Whitman, 2011.
Ages 4–6.

Carly and her older sister, Sandy, love playing in their backyard. Then Lily Jean moves in next door and things change. No longer is Carly an equal in play. Now there's a new dynamic, leaving Carly feeling like an outsider. Without being mean she finds a way to gain her sister's support and teach Lily Jean an important lesson. Like Suzanne Bloom's *What about Bear* (recommended above), this story presents a happy resolution to a situation that takes place whenever several children play together.

6

PLACES NEAR AND FAR

The books in this section take listeners beyond the protective confines of home and family and out into the community. Some go to places just around the corner—a construction site, a museum, around the block or to a firehouse. Others cut across geographical boundaries to enlarge the notion of community and introduce cultural plurality. By tackling universal themes, these titles can enrich a preschooler's worldview and help him or her become more culturally inclusive and better understand what it means to be a respectful citizen of this planet.

AROUND THE CORNER

Around Our Way on Neighbors' Day
By Tameka Fryer Brown. Illustrated by Charlotte Riley-Webb. Abrams, 2010. Ages 4–7.

It's Neighbors' Day, and an energetic little girl is skipping around her multicultural neighborhood spreading the word about the big block party. Old and young, people come out to eat and drink, play ball and chess, and chat while they connect with one another. "Everyone is out to play / Today, around our way." The pictures are alive with energy and detail, giving a wonderful impression of diversity in a city neighborhood.

At the Supermarket

By Anne Rockwell. Illustrated by the author. Holt, 2010. Ages 4–6.

A young boy talks about going to the grocery store with his mother. He likes "the way the door opens all by itself," and helping his mother as she buys all the things they need at home: bread and grapes and peanut butter and toilet paper. They also buy some special things: eggs and flour, sugar and baking powder, and ice cream. The story ends with the mother and child making a cake for the boy's birthday, decorating it with candles they also purchased at the store. In *Put It on the List*, by Kristen Darbyshire, chickens instead of people pilot the shopping cart, and in *Supermarket*, Kathleen Krull describes what goes on behind the scenes at the store.

Bippity Bop Barbershop

By Natasha Anastasia Tarpley. Illustrated by E. B. Lewis. Megan Tingley, 2002. Ages 4–6.

Tarpley focuses on a small but significant event in a child's life. Miles, a young African American boy, is getting his very first haircut. He goes with Dad to a neighborhood barbershop, where the friendly barber greets him, calling him "Little Man." At first tentatively, then with more courage, Miles describes the strange things he sees and what goes on once he climbs into the barber's chair. The best thing of all happens at the end of the visit, when the barber tells Miles, "Guess I can't call you Little Man anymore. . . . You're one of the big boys, now."

Clang! Clang! Beep! Beep! Listen to the City

By Robert Burleigh. Illustrated by Beppe Giacobbe. Simon & Schuster, 2009. Ages 4–6.

In cheerful rhyme, the author, who lives in Chicago, celebrates the sounds a little red-haired boy hears as he goes about his day in the big city. It all begins with the buzzing of the alarm clock. Then come sounds of trash trucks as they pick up their loads, elevated trains clattering above the street, honking horns, buses rumbling, and more. Whimsical cityscapes in bold colors provide a dynamic backdrop for the raucous symphony of sound.

Construction Zone

By Cheryl Willis Hudson. Illustrated with photographs by Richard Sobol.
Candlewick, 2006. Ages 5–7.

From the architect's inception to finishing touch, this full-color photo-essay chronicles the three-year construction of the Massachusetts Institute of Technology Stata Center in Cambridge, Massachusetts. Presenting the project as a gigantic puzzle, the author and photographer examine how the various pieces of brick, steel, cable, and glass fit into the whole, and who works to put them there. Words like *rebar* and *architect* are presented in bold type as they are introduced to listeners and readers. Many children will find it hard to resist those "dozens of people working together to solve a great puzzle."

Farm
By Elisha Cooper. Illustrated by the author. Orchard, 2010. Ages 4–6.

In this glimpse of a modern farm, watercolor illustrations show expansive views of the land and the buildings—the house, the red barn, modern silos—as they appear at each change of season. Small scenes are interspersed throughout, giving a real sense of rural life: chipmunks skitter, cows chew, tractors rumble, "pheasants stalk through the corn." City kids will get a realistic view; rural kids will enjoy seeing what they already know. For a complete change of pace, read Doreen Cronin's boisterous *Click, Clack, Moo: Cows That Type* or *On the Farm*, by David Elliott, a collection of thirteen witty poems.

Firehouse!
By Mark Teague. Illustrated by the author. Scholastic, 2010. Ages 4–6.

Edward, a canine stand-in for a child, and his cousin Judy pay a visit to local firehouse, where firefighters (all dogs except for one mouse) show their visitors around. Edward gets to try on a fire hat and sit behind the wheel of the big truck. When a fire drill causes everyone to hustle, Edward mostly gets in the way. He redeems himself, however, by rescuing a kitty from a tree.

First Day
By Dandi Daley Mackall. Illustrated by Tiphanie Beeke. Harcourt, 2003. Ages 4–6.

Two tiny black dots and a rosebud-shaped squiggle turn a pink daub of paint into a little girl's happy face; rectangles of different colors become a tower of blocks. Using a perfusion of colorful shapes and simple patterns, Beeke shows children enjoying all the activities they might experience during their first day at preschool or kindergarten. In rhyming words, the child describes what she does—from the before-school preparations ("Pencils sharp, crayons stacked. / Ruler, scissors, paper packed") and the "swallow hard" anxieties she feels when she leaves home, to the painting, sliding, and storytelling that fill out her happy day away.

Follow the Line to School

By Laura Ljungkvist. Illustrated by the author. Viking, 2011. Ages 4–6.

Part of a series called Follow the Line, this book conducts children on a verbal and visual tour through an ideal school. A black line marks the path children follow through the school, from the library filled with books and a well-stocked music room to a fully equipped classroom adorned with student artwork. Questions about the pictures pepper the text—"Which book on this page do you think is about baseball?"—inviting both immediate response and further conversation. Ljungkvist uses the same technique to guide children through a house, on a vacation, and around the world.

A Good Night Walk

By Elisha Cooper. Illustrated by the author. Orchard, 2005. Ages 4–6.

Cooper conveys the simple pleasure of a parent and child on an evening walk around the neighborhood. As the stroll begins, an apple pie sits in a window sill, the postman is delivering the mail, boys are mowing a lawn. On the return trip, as the sky darkens, the houses take on a different look; activities of the day are winding down; the moon is beginning to rise, its light shining down on a quieting neighborhood. What seems ordinary becomes almost magical. The figures in the pictures are small, and the details many, making this a candidate better for lap sharing than reading side by side. In other books, Cooper takes readers on trips to the farm, the beach, and a county fair.

Goodnight, Goodnight, Construction Site

By Sherri Duskey Rinker. Illustrated by Tom Lichtenheld. Chronicle, 2011. Ages 4–6.

A construction site may seem an unlikely setting for a bedtime book, but Rinker successfully turns big rigs into sleepyheads. As the sun sets on a construction site, five trucks settle in for the night. The crane folds up, the cement mixer takes a bath, the bulldozer settles down in the dirt, and the other two trucks finish their own nighttime routines. For little ones who can't get enough books about trucks, this one fits the bill.

How the Dinosaur Got to the Museum

By Jessie Hartland. Illustrated by the author. Blue Apple, 2011. Ages 5–7.

On a visit to the Smithsonian, a little boy asks how the museum's *Diplodocus* exhibit came to be. He hears about the many people who worked on the project: the dinosaur hunter, the excavators, the movers, the exhibit designers, the night watchman, and many more. Nicely varied in composition, the artwork offers plenty of details for children to discover. You might also have fun sharing Hartland's *How the Sphinx Got to the Museum.*

How to Make a Cherry Pie and See the U.S.A.
By Marjorie Priceman. Illustrated by the author. Knopf, 2008. Ages 5–7.

In *How to Make an Apple Pie and See the World*, a little girl travels the globe to find the ingredients for her dessert. This time she wants cherry pie for the Fourth of July, but she doesn't have a bowl or a rolling pin or pot holders or a baking pan. As resourceful as ever, she hops in a cab, boards a boat, takes a bus, and makes use of other modes of transport to tour the country to find clay for her mixing bowl (New Mexico), granite for her pastry board (New Hampshire), cotton for her pot holders (Louisiana). What a trip; what a pie. Next stop: the kitchen, where adults and kids can try out the recipe the little girl used. A map tracking the child's journey and lots of landmarks in the pictures add to the fun.

Library Lion
By Michelle Knudsen. Illustrated by Kevin Hawkes. Candlewick, 2006. Ages 4–6.

You would expect the local library to have books and computers. But a lion? One day a lion enters, walking "right past the circulation desk and up into the stacks" Mr. McBee is annoyed, especially when Lion lets out a tremendous ROAR. His boss, Miss Merriweather, is more open to the visitor. There are, after all, no rules about lions. As long as the lion keeps silent, he's welcome. To Mr. McBee's irritation, the lion becomes a library fixture. Then the unexpected happens: the lion roars again.

Mr. Peek and the Misunderstanding at the Zoo
By Kevin Waldron. Illustrated by the author. Templar, 2010. Ages 4–6.

It appears Mr. Peek, the zookeeper, has put on some weight. His tummy protrudes from his favorite uniform jacket! As he makes his rounds he ponders his poundage, feeling more and more sorry for himself as he goes about his rounds. "You're getting very fat," he mumbles as he passes the hippo; while walking by the elephant, he mutters about getting old and wrinkled. Unfortunately, his animal charges jump to the conclusion that he's talking about them. When Mr. Peek discovers he took the wrong uniform jacket off the hook, he's much relieved, and so are his animals.

Our Corner Grocery Store

By Joanne Schwartz. Illustrated by Laura Beingessner. Tundra, 2009. Ages 4–6.

Saturday is Anna Maria's favorite day. It's the day she helps Nonno Domanico and Donna Rosa in their tiny neighborhood market. She likes everything about the day, from her grandfather's hearty *"Buon giorno"* when she arrives early in the morning to the shelves piled high with goods, to the vegetables stacked in wooden bins by the door, to the handwritten signs announcing their prices. She loves the ginger cat with the white tummy, and the umbrellas and shoelaces that hang from the market ceiling. During the day she helps out, but she also has time to play with her friend. Even little listeners who have never seen a mom-and-pop store will find the idea cozy and comforting.

Pizza at Sally's

By Monica Wellington. Illustrated by the author. Dutton, 2006. Ages 4–6.

Sally makes pizza and sells it at her pizzeria. Arriving early every morning, she dons her checkered apron and multicolored chef's hat and begins making the pies. For the sauce, she chops onions and peppers and adds the tomatoes she grows in the community garden. Then she makes the dough. Finally, with her calico cat and eager children looking on, she pops the pies in the oven. Later . . . yum, yum, yum! The pictures add to the fun. Sally works busily on each right-hand page, while the text is on the left, inside a pizza-shaped ring of tiny pictures of ingredients and utensils. By the end of the book, everyone will be ready to try Wellington's pizza recipe.

Sky Boys: How They Built the Empire State Building

By Deborah Hopkinson. Illustrated by James E. Ransome. Schwartz & Wade, 2006. Ages 5–8.

An enthusiastic young boy tells what he sees as he watches the construction of the Empire State Building. What fascinates him the most are the fearless men, the sky boys, who "crawl / like spiders on steel, / spinning their giant web in the sky." From dizzying heights, they maneuver heavy girders into place until the skeleton is ready to receive its outer skin. Finally, when the building opens in 1931, the boy and his father pay a visit. Excited, they ride the elevator to the top, where they "see what the sky boys have seen" for themselves. A salute to the sky boys of today as well as those of times gone by.

To the Beach!

By Linda Ashman. Illustrated by Nadine Bernard Westcott. Harcourt, 2005. Ages 4–6.

It's hot; it's hot; it's oh so hot! So Mom, Dad, and their five youngsters head for the beach. But Katie forgets the dog, Mama runs off without her beach umbrella, and nobody remembers Baby's pail. "Hit the brakes! Reverse the car!" is the lively refrain, and by the time the family gathers up everything they've forgotten, a storm hits. Will they ever make it to the beach? Nope. When the sun comes out, they opt for a great time in their own backyard.

The Village Garage

By G. Brian Karas. Illustrated by the author. Christy Ottaviano, 2010. Ages 4–7.

The cheerful workers at the Village Garage take on different tasks each season. In spring, they clean up debris left over from winter rain and snow. In summer, they patch the streets and interact with the community at a Fourth of July party. In autumn, they collect leaves with a big machine, and in winter, they plow snowy roads. In between, the workers have a little fun. Kids crazy about vehicles will see some not usually mentioned in picture books as well as plenty they see rolling down their neighborhood streets.

AROUND THE WORLD

14 Cows for America

By Carmen Agra Deedy and Wilson Kimeli Naiyomah. Illustrated by Thomas Gonzalez.
Peachtree, 2009. Ages 5–7.

Naiyomah, a Maasai student visiting New York at the time the twin towers were destroyed, returns to his home in Kenya and describes what he saw. To express their sorrow, the people of his homeland donate fourteen cows, symbols of life to the Maasai, to America. A huge crowd, many in ceremonial splendor, greet the ambassador when he comes to accept the Maasai's gift, underscoring that compassion and generosity exist despite global boundaries and cultural divides. Parents and children can find out more about the gift and the givers by visiting the book's website, http://14cowsforamerica.com.

Biblioburro: A True Story from Colombia

By Jeanette Winter. Illustrated by the author. Beach Lane, 2010. Ages 5–7.

Luis loves books, and he wants to share them with others in Colombian mountain villages, where books are rare. With two burros (one loaded with books), he starts his journey. His travels take him across rough terrain; bandits accost him. But eventually he reaches a remote village, unloads his precious cargo, and reads a story to the village children before heading home. While this is a celebration of the pleasures of reading, it's also a reminder of the difference one person can make in the lives of others.

The Biggest Soap

By Carole Lexa Schaefer. Illustrated by Stacey Dressen-McQueen.
Melanie Kroupa, 2004. Ages 4–6.

Set in the island nation of Micronesia, this happy, bubbling tale follows an easily distracted child charged with what seems to be a simple errand. Mama sends Kessy to the store for the "biggest piece of laundry soap." He runs quickly at first, but it isn't long before his attention turns to what's happening along the way: his brothers' games, his uncle at work, his friend with a new camera. He sees the same the people on his way home with the soap, but this time, he stops. His friend needs soap to clean a cut; his brothers need a wash, and his uncle needs soap for his work. By the time he returns home, his soap is only a tiny sliver.

Bikes for Rent!

By Isaac Olaleye. Illustrated by Chris Demarest. Orchard, 2001. Ages 4–7.

This quiet, heartwarming story is set in Nigeria. Lateef longs to join the other boys who ride their bikes around the village, but his parents have no money to spare for bike rental from Babtunde. Not one to give up, he works hard to earn enough to pay Babtunde's fee. He picks mushrooms and collects fire wood in the village, saving his coins in a jar. When he has enough money, he rents a bike. He chooses Babtunde's new red one, but while riding it he succumbs to the temptation to show off and damages the bike. Babtunde is disappointed and angered by Lateef's carelessness, but because he recognizes the boy's regret and admires his perseverance and honesty, he works out a plan for Lateef to make amends.

The Butter Man by Elizabeth Alalou and Ali Alalou

The Butter Man

By Elizabeth Alalou and Ali Alalou. Illustrated by Julie Klear Essakalli.
Charlesbridge, 2008. Ages 5–7.

Framed as a story within a story, this book begins as Baba ("father") recalls an episode from his childhood in Morocco while he goes about preparing a meal for his impatient daughter, Nora. Baba tells Nora that during a famine, Nora's grandfather had to travel far away to make enough to buy food for his starving family. The butter was gone, and soon there would be no bread. To help her young son deal with his hunger, Nora's grandmother tells him to keep an eye out for the Butter Man. He does, and his father returns with needed help. An author's note provides facts on the geography and culture of Baba's homeland.

The Caged Birds of Phnom Penh

By Frederick Lipp. Illustrated by Ronald Himler. Holiday House, 2001. Ages 4–7.

Eight-year-old Ary, who lives in pollution-choked Phnom Penh, has heard about places far away where the air is fresh and birds swoop across the sky. Sadly, the only birds she has ever seen belong to the bird vendor, who keeps them caged. Ary's been told that if she makes a wish and a bird flies free, her wish will come true. She uses her savings to buy a bird, but the bird is too timid to fly. Although Ary is very disappointed, she refuses to give up, and her second bird is different; it flies high and away, free at last, giving Ary hope that someday she will leave too.

Come Fly with Me

By Satomi Ichikawa. Illustrated by the author. Philomel, 2008. Ages 4–6.

Cosmos, a toy plane who lives in Paris, wants to break out of his toy box; it's just too confining. He wants go to Somewhere (else). The building with the big dome he sees from his window looks like a good destination. So Cosmos and his buddy, a stuffed dog named Woggy, fly off, soaring above buildings and streets of the fabled City of Light, taking in the fresh air and freedom. There's trouble along the way (a storm and some pesky birds), but as day breaks, they reach their glorious Somewhere.

The Day of the Dead/El Día de Los Muertos

By Bob Barner. Translated by Teresa Mlawer. Holiday, 2010. Ages 4–6.

This bilingual text follows a family through its preparations and celebration of the Day of the Dead, a Mexican festival during which participants honor their deceased ancestors with "offerings of flowers, sugar skulls, and bread." The English text is rhymed; the translation is not, But no matter which way the text is read aloud, listeners will come away with a real sense of the reason behind this traditional family festival.

Elephant Dance

By Theresa Heine. Illustrated by Sheila Moxley. Barefoot Books, 2004. Ages 4–7.

When Grandfather arrives from India, Ravi asks him about life there. The man describes a sun like "a ferocious tiger" in the sky, snow-covered mountaintops, and elephants decorated for Devali celebrations in brilliantly colored silk howdahs. At the end of the day, Ravi creates an elephant dance on his flute and falls asleep to dreams about an elephant dancing. The scenes alternate between Grandfather's depictions of his homeland and the boy's own family life and traditions.

For You Are a Kenyan Child

By Kelly Cunnane. Illustrated by Ana Juan. Atheneum, 2006. Ages 5–7.

Easily distracted, a Kenyan boy shirks his responsibility to watch his family's herd and wanders off in search of other, more interesting things to do. He has no trouble finding them. There's a cheeky monkey to chase, a village to visit, and friends to play with before he remembers what he should be doing. Through the words of the child in the story, little listeners will find out about life in a traditional Kenyan village and also learn a few Swahili words; a glossary provides pronunciation clues for adults reading the book aloud.

Goal!

By Mina Javaherbin. Illustrated by A. G. Ford. Candlewick, 2010. Ages 5–7.

Ajani, a South African boy who lives in a dangerous shantytown, is overjoyed when he's awarded a regulation soccer ball for success at school. No more kicking the cheap ball he and his friends usually use in their game. After his chores he summons his buddies to try out the gift: "When we play, / we forget to worry." A gang of toughs interrupts their game, but the boy, supported by his friends, uses his knowledge of the game to send the interlopers packing.

Grandma Comes to Stay

By Ifeoma Onyefulu. Illustrated with photographs by the author.
Frances Lincoln, 2010. Ages 4–6.

Three-year-old Stephanie, who lives in Ghana, is looking forward to her grandmother's upcoming visit. When Grandma finally arrives, the two do lots of things together, all captured in photos taken at Stephanie's home in a modern apartment. They share a book; Stephanie shows off her bike-riding skill; and Grandma demonstrates how to wrap a traditional headdress and tells Stephanie a story about a magical drum. The universality of a loving intergenerational relationship comes through clearly in the pictures, which show scenes familiar to children no matter where they live.

Happy Birthday, Jamela!

By Niki Daly. Illustrated by the author. Farrar Straus Giroux, 2006.
Ages 4–6.

Jamela is excited about her upcoming birthday. She goes shopping with her mother and grandmother in the South African city where they live, and she finds the perfect birthday dress. Instead of getting new shoes, though, Mama wants her to wear her sturdy black school shoes; the ones Jamela wants are too expensive. Jamela rebels by decorating her school shoes with beads and sparkles. Mama is angry, but a local merchant loves the shoes and encourages Jamela to make some to sell in the market. Jamela does, and she earns enough money to buy new school shoes as well as the sparkly ones she loves.

I Lost My Tooth in Africa

By Penda Diakité. Illustrated by Baba Wagué Diakité. Scholastic, 2006. Ages 4–6.

Filled with warmth and a sense of the daily life in a far off community, this tale, written when the author was eight years old, is based on what happened to her sister, Amina, when the family left home in Oregon to visit relatives in Bamuko, Mali. Amina has a loose tooth. She wonders if the tooth fairy will visit her if she's so far away from home. Her father reassures her, telling that if she puts her tooth under her pillow, the African tooth fairy will bring her a chicken. The last picture shows the girl, minus a tooth, holding the bird.

Kami and the Yaks

By Andrea Stenn Stryer. Illustrated by Bert Dodson. Bay Otter, 2007. Ages 4–6.

Kami, a deaf boy who lives with his family high in the mountains of Tibet, spots his father and brother searching unsuccessfully for the family's yaks. Not convinced they are going in the right direction, the boy sets out alone, making a treacherous climb, further complicated by a violent storm. His hunch proves correct: he finds the animals, one of which is pinned beneath a rock. Now he must climb down the mountain and somehow make his family understand what he has discovered. Bravery and perseverance win out against an extraordinary combination of odds.

Mirror

By Jeannie Baker. Illustrated by the author. Candlewick, 2010. Ages 4–7.

Although this picture book is mostly wordless, it's still a good book to share with a child. Parallel series of pictures depict the same day in the life of two boys who live far apart: one in a village in Morocco, the other from a city in Australia. Each sets out on a journey with his father on a errand, returning to his family at the end of the day. What the boys have in common is every bit as intriguing as their obvious differences.

Monsoon Afternoon by Kashmira Sheth

Monsoon Afternoon

By Kashmira Sheth. Illustrated by Yoshiko Jaeggi. Peachtree, 2008. Ages 4–6.

Dadaji ("grandfather") is a wonderful playmate for his grandson, who is growing up in India. They go to the swings and race boats. They enjoy watching the peacocks strut about, and they talk together about Dadaji's childhood. What they don't like is being scolded by Dadima ("grandmother") for tracking mud into the house. Clearly love across generations isn't bound by culture or place.

My Father's Shop

By Satomi Ichikawa. Illustrated by the author. Kane/Miller, 2006. Ages 5–7.

Mustafa is overjoyed when his father gives him a brightly colored rug for his own. So excited is he that he charges through the Moroccan marketplace with his possession. Attracted by the rug's bright colors, the rooster cries out, "Kho kho hou houuu." Then tourists intrigued by the spectacle respond by mimicking the rooster's cry in their own language. In Spanish, roosters cry "qui-qui-ri-qui"; in English, they call "cock-a-doodle-do"; and so on. A lesson in cultural differences, surprising and uncomplicated.

My Village: Rhymes from around the World

Edited by Danielle Wright. Illustrated by Mique Moriuchi. Frances Lincoln, 2010. Ages 5–7.

Many countries have nursery rhymes or poems for young children lovingly passed down through generations. Wright has assembled twenty-two in this collection, presenting them in both their original languages and in translated versions. The selections, from countries as far flung as Somoa and Switzerland, range from funny to tender to playful to quaint. All are built around subjects—animals, grandfathers, bath time—familiar to children no matter what country they call home.

New Clothes for New Year's Day

By Hyun-Joo Bae. Illustrated buy the author. Kane/Miller, 2007. Ages 5–7.

A Korean child welcomes the lunar New Year with reverence and eagerness. She will wear new clothes for the occasion. Her elaborate traditional costume has many layers; she must wrap and tie her multicolored jacket correctly, and she must take extra care of her lovely silk pouch, which is said to bring her good luck in the year to come. Bae's colorful yet delicate pictures show the child's struggles to get her garment and accessories just right. At the same time they provide intriguing background on how the New Year is celebrated in another culture.

Ocean's Child

By Christine Ford and Trish Holland. Illustrated by David Diaz. Golden, 2009. Ages 3–6.

In a tranquil bedtime story, an Inuit mother, accompanied by her child snuggly warm in a fur-lined parka, paddles the Arctic Ocean toward home as dusk approaches. As the two glide across the luminescent water, they observe other mother-child animal pairs: dolphins, walruses, polar bears, otters. "To each ocean's child we say good night," croons the Inuit mother to the parade of creatures passing by. Indigenous designs decorate the background and the parkas of both mother and child, connecting the weary travelers to their homeland and their heritage

One World, One Day

By Barbara Kerley. Illustrated with photographs. National Geographic, 2009. Ages 5–7.

In rural China a girl must cross a river on a zip line to get to school; in Madagascar a boy herds zebu. Photos taken in twenty-nine different countries show differences in children's lives, but also make it plain that from breakfast to bedtime, children have surprisingly similar days. "At dawn . . . kids around the world get up, wash up, and celebrate a new day. Porridge. Pancakes. Churros. Toast. Hot sweet tea with plenty of milk. Lots of things taste good for breakfast." Eating, going to school, doing chores, having dinner, sleeping, even dreaming are but a few of the many common activities captured in the stunning photos.

Pemba Sherpa

By Olga Cossi. Illustrated by Gary Bernard. Odyssey, 2009. Ages 4–7.

Yang Ki longs to accompany her older brother, Pemba, on his journey up the mountain to gather firewood. His task is part of his training to become a guide for travelers who climb the Himalayas, something Yang Ki would also like to do. Her bossy brother makes fun of her: it's not a job for girls, he scoffs. But Yang Ki is determined. One day she follows him and saves his life when he slips on the treacherous mountain path. New and old collide in this dramatic story about gender roles, set in a place far removed from the lives of most children.

Rain School

By James Rumford. Illustrated by the author. HMH, 2010. Ages 4–7.

Thomas, who lives in a village in Chad, is ready to start school. But there is no school for him to attend. It was destroyed during the rainy season. The children must rebuild it. They make bricks, build walls and desks, and find out how to make a thatched roof to protect them from the sun. Finally school starts, and the children learn to read and write. As the school year ends, the hard rains return and swamp the school, ensuring students will begin next year by constructing a new one. Inspired by the author's experiences as a Peace Corps volunteer in Chad, *Rain School* takes children to a distant place where learning and school aren't taken for granted.

Subway Ride

By Heather Lynn Miller. Illustrated by Sue Ramá. Charlesbridge, 2009. Ages 5–7.

In this lively picture book, five children board the subway for a trip around the world. They begin in Cairo. They "bump and sway" and "hold on tight." They fly along twisty, mostly underground tracks and glimpse subway stations in Moscow, London, New York, Stockholm—ten different cities in all. When the exciting ride comes to an end, the children still have enough energy for playtime in the open air of the park. The words capture the excitement of the journey, making this ideal for reading aloud.

To Market! To Market!

By Anushka Ravishankar. Illustrated by Emanuele Scanziani. Tara, 2007. Ages 4–6.

A girl and her mother enter a large indoor marketplace in India. The child has some money to spend and is eager to find the perfect thing. Soon she's enthralled by the lovely jewelry, the colorful flowers and fabric, spices, and foods. As she wends her way through the stalls, her imagination takes over: "creeping, creeping, creeping. I am a spy." She's having so much fun that when it's time to leave, she's forgotten to buy her trinket.

The White Nights of Ramadan

By Maha Addasi. Illustrated by Ned Gannon. Boyds Mills, 2008. Ages 5–7.

When Noor, a little girl who lives in Kuwait, sees the almost-full moon rise, she knows it's time to prepare for Girigian, a Muslim celebration that takes place during the month of Ramadan, mostly in nations surrounding the Persian Gulf. She explains the holiday's significance and traditions: the special garments, praying through the day, collecting candy, and delivering baskets of food to the less fortunate. The artwork affords a glimpse of Noor's affectionate family and their home, decorated with exquisite carpets and wall hangings. Addasi was raised in Kuwait, and her final note enriches a tale about one of the Muslim world's many and differing traditions.

7

HAVING FUN

Play is children's work; it not only allows kids to have fun but also gives them a chance to improve problem-solving skills, exercise their imaginations, develop friendships, and learn to compromise and follow instructions. The books below touch on a variety of ways to have fun, while tapping into a child's inherently playful nature. Bats play midnight baseball, a girl chases chickens, crocodiles go camping, and everybody comes out for a wild block party. Take your pick.

Alex and the Wednesday Chess Club
By Janet S. Wong. Illustrated by Stacey Schuett. Margaret K. McElderry. Ages 5–7.

When he's soundly beaten at chess by old Hooya, four-year-old Alex gives up the game. After he's sidelined from football in third grade, he joins the chess club and rediscovers his ability. Then it's practice, practice, practice in preparation for his first tournament—only to be faced with the specter of his devastating defeat when Hooya's nephew becomes his opponent. In conversational language that lends itself to reading aloud, Wong melds the story of a boy's discovery of a particular passion with the recognition that winning isn't everything.

The Basket Ball
By Esmé Raji Codell. Illustrated by Jennifer Plecas. Abrams, 2011. Ages 4–6.

Lulu may be dressed like a princess on the cover of this book, but she would rather play with a basketball than with dolls or a magic wand.

Still, the boys on the basketball team are having none of it; they don't want her around. Undaunted, Lulu decides to hold a Basket Ball, and when other girls who show up want to play, they form a team of their own. An empowering book for little girls, whatever their dreams. *Players in Pigtails* by Shana Corey (below), set in a time gone by, is another glimpse of a girl whose first love is baseball.

Bats at the Ballgame

By Brian Lies. Illustrated by the author. Houghton Mifflin, 2010. Ages 4–6.

The author of *Bats at the Beach* and *Bats in the Library* transfers his winged characters' allegiance to the ballpark. With glowing wings, bats grab their bats and "hustle out to diamond sky" to play a grand game. They swoop and glide across the field as fans, hanging upside down on the bleachers, cheer them on. Along with fanciful depictions of the batters up swinging high and low, Lies adds a multitude of comic touches (mothdogs, anyone?) for parents and children to search out in the pictures. It's an exuberant spin on America's greatest pastime—fun for game fans but also for children who have yet to step foot in a stadium.

Batter Up Wombat

By Helen Lester. Illustrated by Lynn Munsinger. Houghton Mifflin, 2006. Ages 4–6.

Their team name may be the Champs, but champions they aren't. They finished dead last in the National Wildlife League. When an Australian wombat (whose name they mistakenly think is "Whambat") appears, they think winning's in the bag. After all, with a name like Whambat, the new guy must be a super hitter. That first goofy mistake is further complicated by Wombat's own linguistic difficulties and his truly dreadful playing skills. Obviously he's not the savior his team envisioned, and he's sad when they are disappointed. Wombat isn't entirely without talents, however. He's very good at digging, and when a tornado threatens the players, he makes a tunnel to keep everyone safe. He still can't play ball, but he's a hero all the same. Lester and Munsinger have a long list of wonderful picture books, most of which use humor to help kids build confidence. Try the Tacky the Penguin books next.

Block Party Today!

By Marilyn Singer. Illustrated by Stephanie Roth. Knopf, 2004. Ages 5–7.

Everyone is excited by the thought of a block party except Lola. She's had a tiff with her friends Yasmin and Sue, and she isn't in the mood for fun. But the lively crowds in the city neighborhood, the music, and

Bats at the Ballgame by Brian Lies

the smells of the food are too enticing to ignore. When Lola's friends spot her outside, they approach her, and friendship wins out over hurt feelings. "No cars! No trucks! Time to run in the street! Time to play double Dutch" and have fun with friends at a great block party.

Callie Cat, Ice Skater

By Eileen Spinelli. Illustrated by Anne Kennedy. Albert Whitman, 2007. Ages 4–6.

Callie Cat loves to ice skate. She loves it "more than chocolate cake," and more than her bright red snowflake sweater. When Honeybrook Ice Rink sponsors a contest, she decides to enter. Callie dutifully listens to all the advice she's given, but though she works very hard, she doesn't win. One day, when her friends aren't around, she goes to the pond and slips on her skates. When she hears "the sun-dazzled blades crisping across the ice," she suddenly understands what was missing from her performance—joy. Winning isn't everything.

Camping Day

By Patricia Lakin. Illustrated by Scott Nash. Dial, 2009. Ages 4–6.

Crocodile buddies Sam, Pam, Will, and Jill enthusiastically venture into the woods for a sure-to-be-great campout. They look forward to roasting marshmallows, telling stories, and singing camp songs. Their reality is somewhat different. Bees, a reluctant campfire, too many beans for supper ("P.U."), and scary noises prove too much for the inept reptiles, who finally decide there's nothing as good as a campout in the backyard. Lakin's cheerful croc quartet appears in several equally funny outings, including *Beach Day!* and *Snow Day!*

The Chicken-Chasing Queen of Lamar County

By Janice N. Harrington. Illustrated by Shelley Jackson. Farrar Straus Giroux, 2007.
Ages 4–6.

Chickens, watch out! The little girl who narrates this comical story has her eye on you. Actually, Miss Hen is her preferred target, and unfortunately for the determined chicken chaser, Miss Hen is a terrific runner and goes into hiding. Big Mama forbids chicken chasing, but how can the little girl be the best chicken chaser if she doesn't practice? It's all very frustrating. When the girl finally finds Miss Hen—on a nest with a brood of fuzzy chicks—she decides to leave off chasing chickens and raise them instead.

Clever Jack Takes the Cake

By Candace Fleming. Illustrated by G. Brian Karas. Schwartz & Wade, 2010. Ages 4–7.

The princess is turning ten, and Jack receives an invitation to her birthday celebration. Parties are fun, but birthdays mean presents—and Jack can't afford one. Instead he makes a luscious layer cake. But pesky blackbirds, a troll, and even a palace guard stop Jack along the way, each taking a piece of the present. By the time Jack gets to the party, the only thing left to give the princess is the story of his travels—which, she assures him, is the best gift of all.

A Couple of Boys Have the Best Week Ever

By Marla Frazee. Illustrated by the author. Harcourt, 2008. Ages 5–7.

James and Eamon, a couple of energetic cartoon buddies, are staying with Eamon's grandparents while attending a week of nature camp during the day: "They miss their parents like crazy (yeah, right)." Grandma Pam makes them waffles and smiles a lot. Grandpa Bill tries to interest them in bird-watching. The boys make faces at each other instead. At camp they throw pinecones and occasionally hang upside down by their feet. They both wear bandages on their foreheads, and they lie in the grass and do nothing at all. What they get out of the week isn't what the grown-ups envisioned, but it's fun, fun, fun all the same.

Dino-Baseball
By Lisa Wheeler. Illustrated by Barry Gott. Carolrhoda, 2010. Ages 4–6.

It's a sunny day at Jurassic Park, and enthusiastic crowds fill the bleachers. The Rib-Eye Reds (carnivores) and the Green Sox (herbivores) are in a playoff. The players are primed and ready to go; it's prehistoric rivalry taken to new heights. Triceratops is up to bat; T-Rex is pitching. The crowd goes wild. A seventh inning stretch, and the game continues; Apatosaurus is the Green Sox's "only hope." Which team will win? Two favorites themes combine in one funny, action-packed read-aloud. *Dino-Soccer, Dino-Hockey,* and the latest book, *Dino-Basketball,* follow the same successful formula.

Dinosaur Dinosaur
By Kevin Lewis. Illustrated by Daniel Kirk. Orchard, 2006. Ages 4–6.

The catchy jump-rope jingle "Teddy Bear, Teddy Bear" is the inspiration for another lively read-aloud about prehistoric critters at play. Comic details in the pictures add to the fun as the book follows a dinosaur kid as he wakes, outfits himself in jeans and a red ball cap, eats his Dino Puffs (his mother reads the *Dinosaur Times*), and joins his buddies, an orange triceratops and a purple brontosaurus, playing soccer and jumping rope: "Busy-whizzy *dinosaur,* / all the livelong day!" Just like human kids everywhere.

Dragon Dancing
By Carole Lexa Schaefer. Illustrated by Pierr Morgan. Viking, 2007. Ages 4–6.

After hearing a story about a dragon, a group of schoolchildren, encouraged by pigtailed Mei Li, uses colored paper, feathers, and sparkles to build a dragon with "boink-boink" eyes and a long ribbon tail. Soon they are out the door with their creation, dragon dancing on a playground transformed by imagination. Like *The Squiggle,* in which a simple piece of red string inspires imaginative play, this book is a beguiling celebration of the delight children find in the simplest things. Brimming with colorful language ("swirl-whirling," "la-dee-daw dawdling"), it is also an excellent choice for little ones.

Drum City
By Thea Guidone. Illustrated by Vanessa Newton. Tricycle, 2010. Ages 4–6.

It begins with one small boy beating out a jaunty rhythm on a pot. Soon others respond to his swingin' sound. With brooms and cans, spoons and

bowls, they flood the city with lively music. No one can resist the synco-
pated beat, and heads turn to watch as the endless line of happy kids, black
and white, big and small, short and tall, follow the drummer boy down the
street. The book's rollicking rhyme begs to be read aloud, possibly accompanied by the beat of a listener's homemade drum.

Easy as Pie

By Cari Best. Illustrated by Melissa Sweet. Farrar Strauss Giroux, 2010. Ages 4–6.

Jacob, who brandishes a wooden spoon in his baby picture, loves to cook.
He especially likes television food celebrity Chef Monty. After watching
Baking with Chef Monty, Jacob decides to bake an anniversary gift for his
parents—a peach pie. Sunny artwork pictures his devotion to Monty's
rules, the most important, perhaps, being "Don't give up." Jacob doesn't,
and he ends up with a delicious Happy Peach Pie, which everyone eats
before dinner. Chef Monty's list of rules and a recipe for pie complete
this delectable story.

Five Little Monkeys Play Hide and Seek

By Eileen Christelow. Illustrated by the author. Clarion, 2004. Ages 4–6.

The naughty monkeys (whose previous, equally hysterical adventures
have taken them from baking a cake to unsuccessfully doing nothing)
cause havoc once again, this time by hiding from their babysitter, Lulu.
Although they promise Mama they'll be good, they can't resist a trick or
two. After a few exemplary rounds of hide-and-seek, the monkeys van-
ish. Lulu is stumped, and she starts to worry. Where could they be? They
are in the very last place anyone (except Mama) would look: in bed. Rollicking fun; good for counting practice, too.

Follow the Leader

By Erica Silverman. Illustrated by G. Brian Karas. Farrar Straus and Giroux, 2003. Ages 4–6.

Big Brother insists that Little Brother copy whatever he says and does.
After patiently following along, Little Brother has had enough. His idea
of fun isn't (literally) jumping through hoops. He wants to try his hand
at being a leader, too, and rather than end the game, Big Brother agrees.
It's plain from the impish expression on Little Brother's face when he
takes over the lead that he has sweet revenge in mind.

Hot Rod Hamster

By Cynthia Lord. Illustrated by Derek Anderson. Scholastic, 2010. Ages 4–6.

Hamster has a "need for speed," and 4 Paws Speedway is the place to go. But before he can take to the track, he needs a car. With help from a bunch of mice and a junkyard bulldog (who asks listeners to select the parts of the car), he builds one. It's a beauty, too— an "itty-bitty green car," decorated with orange flames. Next it's off to the track, where Hamster is up against a crew of determined dogs. Winning isn't his only concern. If he crosses the finish line first, which trophy should he choose? For other stories about hot-wheel wonders, look for Alex Zane's *Wheels on the Race Car* and Kristy Dempsey's *Mini Racer* at your library.

How Do You Wokka-Wokka?

By Elizabeth Bluemle. Illustrated by Randy Cecil. Candlewick, 2009. Ages 4–6.

What's a "wokka-wokka?" Think of it as happy nonsense. As a boy travels through his urban neighborhood, he asks everyone he passes how they do their wokka-wokka. Everyone he asks has a "wokka way," which always involves flapping, dancing, and hopping around, as well as some delightfully silly rhyme and wordplay. A wild party on the "blocka-blocka" is the end result. Tongue-twisting fun, guaranteed to inspire energetic leaping around as well as some original nonsense rhymes.

How to Catch a Fish

By John Frank. Illustrated by Peter Sylvada. Neal Porter, 2007. Ages 5–7.

Fishing isn't high on the list of common topics for children's book authors, though it's an activity shared by many parents and children. This collection of thirteen linked poems gives the sport its due. To answer the title question, the book traverses the globe from Japan to Ireland to Namibia to New England, to introduce various forms fishing takes: ice fishing, seine fishing, spearfishing, fly-fishing, and more. Adults and children who enjoy this pastime will be well pleased.

I Ain't Gonna Paint No More!

By Karen Beaumont. Illustrated by David Catrow. Harcourt, 2005. Ages 4–6.

Written to the tune of Wendell Hall's 1923 song "It Ain't Gonna Rain No Mo!" this raucous tale speaks to parents as well as kids. "Ya ain't a-gonna paint no more!" declares Mama, who confiscates her son's supplies and plops him in the tub. Unfortunately, that's not sufficient to stem the little guy's creative drive. After liberating his paints, he proceeds to "take some red / and I paint my . . . / HEAD!" following up by painting other parts of his body until he's a human rainbow. Just when it seems he's painted everything there is he finds one last thing: "I'm such a nut, / gonna paint my— / WHAT?!" Whether the words are read aloud or sung, kids will catch on to the repetition and rhyme very quickly and enjoy completing the verses themselves.

Jazzmatazz!
By Stephanie Calmenson. Illustrated by Bruce Degen. HarperCollins, 2008. Ages 4–6.

To escape the cold of a wintry day, Mouse slips into a house, spots a piano, and starts tippy-tapping a jazzy tune on the keys. Dog grabs his bone; cat grabs a spoon, and the bird adds a warble or two. Soon Baby joins in, dancing to the beat; dad starts to whistle; Mom begins to clap; and pretty soon even the neighbors are swinging to the music. Everyone's dancing, singing, and having a terrific time. Looking for books on other types of music? Try *Rock 'n' Roll Mole* by Carolyn Crimi, *Little Pig Joins the Band* by David Hyde Costello, or Lloyd Moss's award-winning *Zin! Zin! Zin! A Violin.*

Let's Do Nothing!
By Tony Fucile. Illustrated by the author. Candlewick, 2009. Ages 4–6.

Eyeing the games, puzzles, toys, balls, and books strewn around the bedroom, a red-haired cartoon kid named Sal and his bespectacled little buddy, Frankie, decide they've pretty much done everything there is to do. In a moment of sheer genius Sal decides they should sit absolutely still: be statues. Unfortunately, Frankie fares poorly at this do-nothing business (pigeons and dogs are involved), but his experience eventually pushes Sal toward another bright idea: find something else to do.

Madlenka Soccer Star
By Peter Sís. Illustrated by the author. Farrar Straus Giroux, 2010. Ages 5–7.

Imaginative Madelenka spreads her enthusiasm for soccer throughout her neighborhood and throughout the world. Her search for a playmate begins on her street. What about a dog, some cats, or a parking meter with legs? In her fantasy, she journeys far away, encountering other children who love the sport as much as she does. In the end, she returns home, where her best friend and other children from her neighborhood gather to play. A historical note about the game appears on the last page, along with a look at the word *soccer* as it is written in more than forty different languages. Build in lots of time to look at Sís's pictures; they are chockablock with meticulously drafted details that enrich the story. Look for other books about the imaginative little girl: *Madelenka*, in which Madelenka advertises to the world that her tooth is loose, and *Madelenka's Dog*, costarring Madelenka's canine pal.

Never Take a Shark to the Dentist (and Other Things Not to Do)
By Judi Barrett. Illustrated by John Nickle. Atheneum, 2008. Ages 4–6.

In a delightfully droll bit of nonsense, the author of *Cloudy with a Chance of Meatballs* turns from pasta, potatoes, and pancakes to pelicans, pigeons, porcupines, and others from the animal kingdom. Don't sit next to a porcupine; don't take a giraffe to the movies, and "never take a shark to the dentist!" are among Barrett's bits of sage advice, all accompanied by pictures that demonstrate the consequences of not paying attention. It won't be long before adults and kids will be inventing their own crazy scenarios—skunks and pigs will surely come to mind.

Nothing to Do
By Douglas Wood. Illustrated by Wendy Anderson Halperin. Dutton 2006. Ages 5–7.

Wood offers a more serene vision of downtime than Fucile does in his tongue-in-cheek *Let's Do Nothing* (above), although he agrees with Fucile in his underlying theme: there's never nothing to do. Computer games and the like aren't mentioned. Instead, Wood references quieter pursuits—making models, sipping lemonade, hiking, and spending quiet moments daydreaming—as the best opportunities to have fun and escape the hectic pace of modern life. It's all about slowing down and learning to appreciate the world in a new way.

Pig Kahuna
By Jennifer Sattler. Illustrated by the author. Bloomsbury, 2011. Ages 4–6.

Pigs are popping up everywhere in picture books these days. They even go to the beach. Fegus the piglet hates water but loves beachcombing. He and his little brother, Dink, have collected a quite a few exciting things. One day, the best thing ever washes ashore: an abandoned surfboard. The board, which the boys name Dave, becomes the centerpiece of their col-

Pig Kahuna by Jennifer Sattler

lection. When Dink feels sorry for keeping the board in captivity and sets
it free, Fegus must overcome his fear of the ocean to recover it. To his
great surprise, he discovers that riding the waves can be exciting and fun.

A Pig Parade Is a Terrible Idea

By Michael Ian Black. Illustrated by Kevin Hawkes. Simon & Schuster, 2010. Ages 4–7.

Everyone loves a parade, so what's wrong with a having a pig parade? Ask
the pigs. They'll tell you. While some pictures show cartoony porcines in
colorful band uniforms marching and tooting away on trumpets, others
show pigs in their natural element, chomping away on whatever catches
their attention. Listeners will get an earful. It will be hard not to think
of pigs the next time a parade passes by.

Pirate Boy

By Eve Bunting. Illustrated by Julie Fortenberry. Holiday House, 2011. Ages 4–6.

After reading a picture book called *Pirate Boy* together, Danny and his
mom create their own pirate adventure. As confident and enthusiastic as
he is about heading off on the high seas, Danny is still very glad to have

Mom on hand when he encounters some unfriendly pirates and a couple of threatening sea monsters. Given the popularity of pirates these days, children might also like *Pirates Don't Take Baths* by John Segal, *How I Became a Pirate* by Melinda Long, and *Pirate Girl* by Cornelia Funke.

Players in Pigtails

By Shana Corey. Illustrated by Rebecca Gibbon. Scholastic, 2003. Ages 5–7.

Katie, growing up during the 1940s, is not like other girls she knows. She doesn't enjoy cooking or needlework, and she can't dance. She loves baseball; pitching, catching, fielding, and batting are all she thinks about. She isn't allowed to play with the boys on the school team, but she perseveres and earns a cherished spot on a team in the newly organized All-American Girls Professional Baseball League. Katie is fictional, but the league really existed, and enthusiastic sports fans packed the games. This tribute to the league and to the resolute women who played for it brings baseball history within reach of today's young sports fans.

Pretend

By Jennifer Plecas. Illustrated by the author. Philomel, 2011. Ages 4–6.

Like Eve Bunting's *Pirate Boy* (above), this book is about a parent and a child engaged in creative play. Familiar objects in their cozy house provide the springboard for a father and son to devise an adventure. The sofa becomes a boat, the stairs become a mountain, and the family dog becomes the trusted sidekick as the pair slips out of reality and ventures forth to explore an island far, far from home. Those who already know the magical properties of pillow forts and blanket caves will feel right at home.

Rattletrap Car

By Phyllis Root. Illustrated by Jill Barton. Candlewick, 2001. Ages 4–6.

Everybody is hot, even the baby, so Papa suggests a trip to the lake. The family gathers its sand and sun gear—including a surfboard, a beach ball, and a bucket full of sticky fudge—and gets into its old jalopy. They don't get far before a tire goes flat. Clever little Junie puts things right (using the beach ball and some fudge), and the family continues on its way. After several equally goofy roadside emergencies, they reach the pond— but how in the world will their rattletrap car get home again?

Ready, Set, Skip!

By Jane O'Connor. Illustrated by Ann James. Viking, 2007. Ages 4–6.

A child watches her classmates skipping. She wants to skip, too, but she doesn't know how. She can do many other things, like twirl and jump and even roller skate, all of which she demonstrates to her devoted dog. Dog is no help, though, when it comes to figuring out how to skip—but her mother is. Rhyming verses keep the text moving briskly along while never making light of the child's many feelings. This will be especially encouraging to the child whose motor skills haven't quite caught up to those of the rest of the pack.

Roller Coaster

By Marla Frazee. Illustrated by the author. Harcourt, 2003. Ages 5–7.

They are fat; they are thin; they are young; they are old. They are all in line, patiently waiting their turn to ride the roller coaster. The words rising, falling, coiling, following the path of the cars as they go up, "clickity, clackity / clickity, clackity," all the way to the top. Then the roller coaster plunges downward, its passengers open-mouthed, excited, and terrified at the same time. What a thrill!

Sergio Saves the Game!

By Edel Rodriguez. Illustrated by the author. Little, Brown, 2009. Ages 4–6.

A penguin named Sergio loves soccer. In his dreams he's a terrific player, celebrated by his teammates. In reality, he's not so hot. In fact he's a mess, and he's the last player chosen for a team. Determined not to let his teammates down during the big game with the Seagulls, he practices. Day and night, with his red scarf billowing out behind him, he dribbles, and kicks, and shoots. And in the end, he scores. *Big Kicks* by Bob Kolar is another good soccer story for the preschool kindergarten audience.

Shark vs. Train

By Chris Barton. Illustrated by Tom Lichtenheld. Little, Brown, 2010. Ages 4–6.

Having each picked a formidable combatant from the toy box, two red-haired boys are primed for fun and action. One boy wields a stuffed shark with a malicious toothy grin; the other is armed with an awesome toy train. I'm going to "choo" you up, snarls the shark, while the train bellows out his own warning, which involves "fin-ishing" off his opponent. Hysterical wordplay and funny cartoon illustrations track the combat, which gets sillier and sillier as each ferocious warrior jockeys for the upper hand.

Tacky Goes to Camp
By Helen Lester. Illustrated by Lynn Munsinger. Houghton Mifflin, 2009. Ages 4–6.

Ah, summer camp in snow land—Camp Whoopihah to be exact. Penguin campers Goodly, Lovely, Angel, Neatly, and Perfect are prepared. Their names are neatly sewn on their camp shirts. They have their sleeping bags, their regulation tents, and other camping gear. They are ready to go. Tacky is odd penguin out. He's brought his bunny slippers and his pillow, and his yellow-and-orange striped tent, complete with an antennae for his TV, is more appropriate for a trip to the circus. Tacky's approach to camp activities (like synchronized swimming) is equally nontraditional, but when a bear threatens the campsite, Tacky finds a resourceful way to save the day.

To the Big Top
By Jill Esbaum. Illustrated by David Gordon. Farrar Straus Giroux, 2008. Ages 4–6.

In days gone by, two boys, Sam and Benny, witness the arrival of a traveling circus in their small town. Thrilled, they watch as the animals, tents, and other equipment are unloaded. When a workman invites them to help with the setup, they happily agree, lugging water and pitching hay. For their work each boy receives a nickel and a highly prized ticket to the show. Then a monkey makes off with Sam's ticket, and two friends must quickly find a way to get it back. Adult readers might want to share facts about the old-fashioned big top included in an author's note.

Too Many Toys
By David Shannon. Illustrated by the author. Blue Sky, 2008. Ages 4–6.

Is there such a thing as "too many toys"? Spencer's mother thinks so, as she surveys Spencer's overflowing room and follows a trail of toys through the house. Puzzles and robots, beach balls and skateboards, and puppets and games are scattered everywhere. It's abundantly clear that some weeding is in order. Ignoring Spencer's stubborn commitment to his collection, his exhausted mother gathers a box of giveaways—only to have Spencer gleefully announce that the *box* is his favorite toy of all. Shannon, the author of *Oh, David!* and other books about a naughty but loveable kid with long-suffering parents, invests Spencer with the same kind of irrepressible energy and mischief. Both parents and kids will probably recognize bits of themselves as they read.

Traction Man Meets Turbo Dog

By Mini Grey. Illustrated by the author. Knopf, 2008. Ages 4–6.

The ruggedly handsome, square-jawed action figure—introduced in *Traction Man Is Here*— returns, fresh from besting evildoers like Poisonous Dishcloth, a wicked garden spade, and other villains that lurk around the house. This time "brave little scrubbing brush," Traction Man's devoted sidekick, is in jeopardy. The more hygienic battery-operated Turbo Dog is primed to take his place—but not if Traction Man has anything to say about it. Fun, absolutely, but like Chris Barton's *Shark vs. Train* (above), this is also an astute tale about children's imaginations at work. For more superhero fun, try Michael Chabon's *Astonishing Secret of Awesome Man.*

The Turkey Bowl

By Phil Bildner. Illustrated by C. F. Payne. Simon & Schuster, 2008. Ages 4–7.

Every Thanksgiving, Ethan's relatives come to his house to play football. This year he's finally old enough to join them. To his great disappointment, a blizzard has closed the roads, keeping his relatives away. When he ventures outdoors, however, he finds enough neighborhood kids to start his own Turkey Bowl on the snowy outdoor field. In the end, just as he catches a winning pass, he realizes his family was able to come after all, and they are all lined up watching him play. Even though the pictures have a nostalgic feel, the tale still speaks to sports fans of today.

We All Move

By Rebecca Rissman. Illustrated with photographs. Heinemann Library, 2009. Ages 4–6.

Climbing, dancing, jumping, racing, riding, running, skiing, swimming, and walking—people are always on the move. Each page has one simple sentence accompanied by a photo of someone moving for exercise or just for fun.

8

MAKING BELIEVE

Role-playing games are an integral part of childhood. They allow preschoolers to escape from the mostly literal way they see the world and try on different hats; they tug at the imagination. Picture book stories are a little like role-playing games. They sweep listeners from their comfortable spot on the couch—or the bed, or the reading rug—to a different place. The titles in this section go a tiny step further; they feast on the impossible. Magical, mysterious, improbable, fantastic, they encourage children to delve deeply into their imaginations, think creatively, and accept that absolutely anything can happen in books.

April and Esme: Tooth Fairies

By Bob Graham. Illustrated by the author. Candlewick, 2010. Ages 4–6.

April is a tooth fairy, but her parents think she and little sister Esme are too young to do the job. When Daniel Dangerfield loses his tooth, the girls see their chance to try their wings. Their parents eventually concede defeat and send the girls off, Daniel's coin in a string bag dangling between them. They narrowly escape being caught, but to everyone's delight their first mission is a success. Don't expect frilly fairies in pink tutus here. Mom and Dad are winged throwbacks to the 1960s, while Esme wears big glasses and April has a cell phone. Their house is unexpected, too: the nightstand is a thimble; teeth are strung from the ceiling. What is conventional is the underlying message about children needing space to grow up, presented by Graham in fresh, funny, whimsical fashion.

Billy Twitters and His Blue Whale Problem

By Mac Barnett. Illustrated by Adam Rex. Hyperion, 2009. Ages 5–7.

Billy has failed to clean his room, and his parents (whose faces are never shown) demand reform. They devise a plan to make him more responsible. The "plan" arrives in a FedUP truck. It is an enormous blue whale, which Billy must care for and take along wherever he goes. His parents are no help—and neither is the owner's manual. Obviously Billy Twitters is in *big* trouble. The pictures increase the laughs. Cats follow along as Billy drags his enormous whale burden down the street, the Golden Gate Bridge in the background. The superb nonsense continues to the very last page.

Bubble Trouble

By Margaret Mahy. Illustrated by Polly Dunbar. Clarion, 2008. Ages 4–6.

Mabel blows a bubble big enough to surround her baby brother. The cherry-cheeked child floats out the window and over the town, gathering a parade of gawkers who monitor the bubble's wibble-wobbling, bibble-bobbling progress. In the meantime, the thoroughly delighted baby, who usually appears in the upper right-hand corner of each picture spread, floats higher and higher. Reaching Baby with a human ladder doesn't work, but a pebble loosed by an old-fashioned slingshot sure does. Tongue-twisting language and jolly rhymes work wonderfully with the amusing pictures and the imaginative take on brother-sister relationships.

By the Light of the Harvest Moon

By Harriet Ziefert. Illustrated by Mark Jones. Blue Apple, 2009. Ages 4–6.

As the light of day disappears, a fantastical autumn festival begins. Red, yellow, and orange leaves, carried by the wind, settle on the ground, only to spring back to life as leafy grown-ups and children who are poised to celebrate fall. In hats and jackets and shoes, the leaf children have races, bob for apples, and play children's games. In the end, they eat some delicious pie, and having had fun all day, join their families for a nighttime sail in the breeze. Lois Ehlert's *Leaf Man*, a more naturalistic glimpse of fall leaves, includes an identification guide.

Chalk

By Bill Thomson. Illustrated by the author. Marshall Cavendish, 2010. Ages 5–7.

Three children visiting the park on a rainy day find an intriguing bag of colored chalk. When the first child draws a sun, the clouds miraculously disappear and the sun comes out. When the second child draws butterflies, gorgeous monarchs fill the air. The third child draws a dinosaur. Oops! Thomson's amazing photo-realistic illustrations communicate the entire story, which allows onlookers to create their own version of the magical goings-on.

The Day Ray Got Away

By Angela Johnson. Illustrated by Luke LaMarca. Simon & Schuster, 2010. Ages 4–6.

Ray, a giant yellow parade-balloon sun, is tired of floating above the crowds and then returning to the balloon warehouse to wait until the next parade. He yearns to fly free, and he has developed a plan. Putting his idea into action, he leaves his stunned balloon buddies behind, the strings tethering him to Earth getting longer and longer while he gets smaller. As Ray disappears into the sky, the crowds below gasp, and the other parade balloons begin thinking up their own ways to escape.

The Dollhouse Fairy

By Jane Ray. Illustrated by the author. Candlewick, 2009. Ages 4–6.

In this reassuring tale, magic helps a little girl face a difficult situation in her life. On Saturdays Rosy and Dad work on her dollhouse. They make up stories and construct new objects for the make-believe family that lives there. Then her father goes to the hospital. When Rosy next looks into the dollhouse she finds Thistle, a mischievous fairy with a broken wing. Rosy cares for Thistle until she's able to fly—just as Daddy is cared for until he's able to come home. Rosy looks forward to introducing Dad to the secret visitor, only to find that Thistle, like an imaginary friend no longer needed, has disappeared.

Flora's Very Windy Day

By Jeanne Birdsall. Illustrated by Matt Phelan. Clarion, 2010. Ages 4–6.

Flora is angry and frustrated when her toddler brother, Crispin, upsets her things again. She complains to Mom, who sends both children outdoors to settle down. A sudden, surprisingly strong wind lifts frightened Crispin into the air. Flora grabs his hand, and the two float upward on the current. Each fellow sky traveler they encounter—among them, a dragonfly, a sparrow, and a cloud—offers to take charge of Flora's annoying brother, but Flora's heart tells her not to let him go. Despite his irritating behavior she still loves him.

Flotsam

By David Wiesner. Illustrated by the author. Clarion, 2006. Ages 5–8.

In this wordless book, a curious boy goes beachcombing. He finds a cam-

Flotsam by David Wiesner

era—not just any camera, an old one with a roll of film yet to be developed. And what pictures they turn out to be . . . starfish walking upright along the beach; tiny underwater aliens in blue suits. Most intriguing of all, though, is the picture of a little girl holding the photo of another child, who took a picture of himself, just as the little girl did, before passing on the camera. After taking his own photo, the boy tosses the camera back into the ocean, where it will surely end up in the hands of another curious child. Each illustration begs a story all its own. In *Tuesday*, another virtually wordless book by Wiesner, flying frogs make a surprise visit to a sleepy town.

Franklin's Big Dreams
By David Teague. Illustrated by Boris Kulikov. Hyperion, 2010. Ages 4–6.

The magic and mystery of dreams is the heart of this unusual bedtime book. One night a construction crew crashes through Franklin's bedroom wall. After train tracks take shape, the boy and his dog witness a train hurtling through the room. Curiously, nothing remains of the exciting events when the sun comes up, but the crew returns on subsequent nights to build a runway and a waterway. If having a train, a ship, and airplane in one's room weren't remarkable enough, each conveyance carries passengers who look very familiar to Franklin—especially one particular little boy and his distinctive little dog.

Ginger and Petunia
By Patricia Polacco. Illustrated by the author. Philomel, 2007. Ages 5–7.

A celebrated musician, Virginia Vincent Folsum loves turbans, floaty scarves, lots of beads, and her little red sports car. She also loves her pet pig, Petunia, who lives a life of luxury right along with her eccentric owner. Petunia even has her own mudhole. Called to London to perform a concert, Ginger kisses Petunia goodbye and leaves, confident her house sitter will handle everything that comes along. When the sitter suddenly cancels, Petunia raids Ginger's closet and takes on the role of socialite and mistress of the house—with hilarious results.

The Gold Miner's Daughter: A Melodramatic Fairy Tale
By Jackie Mims Hopkins. Illustrated by Jon Goodell. Peachtree, 2006. Ages 4–7.

Hopkins ushers listeners right into her story, asking them to pretend they are watching an old Western that requires hissing and booing on cue. The movie plot may seem familiar: Gracie Pearl and her dad owe a bunch of money to their villainous, mustachioed landlord. But valiant Gracie is convinced there's gold in "them thar hills," and she sets out to find it. Factor in some fairy tale characters—including Sleeping Beauty and the Three Little Pigs—who are also searching for gold, and you have a wacky, interactive story, ideal for involving kids in the reading experience.

The Great Fuzz Frenzy
By Janet Stevens and Susan Stevens Crummel. Illustrated by Janet Stevens. Harcourt, 2005. Ages 4–6.

Fuzz is the star of this wacky adventure, which requires total suspension of disbelief. When Violet the dog innocently drops a fuzzy green tennis ball down a prairie dog hole, she incites a rodent riot. Everyone wants piece of the fuzz, especially bullying king dog Big Bark, who grabs most of the goods. Horizontal and vertical foldout pages that explore the down under of prairie dog digs add to the inventive hullabaloo.

The House in the Night
By Susan Marie Swanson. Illustrated by Beth Krommes. Houghton Mifflin, 2008. Ages 4–6.

"In the house / burns a light. / In that light / rests a bed. On that bed / waits a book." In the tradition of the "House that Jack Built," this imaginative tale follows a young girl who enters a house with a key and finds an open book. From the book hops a bird, which conducts the girl on a journey through a sky twinkling with stars straight to a smiling moon. Precisely detailed scratchboard illustrations, touched with golden highlights, show a neatly ordered house and a neatly ordered bedroom, a teddy bear and the open book sharing space with a violin on the cozy coverlet. As individual as snowflakes, stars light the way for the child's nighttime journey.

How the Moon Regained Her Shape

By Janet Ruth Heller, Illustrated by Ben Hodson. Sylvan Dell, 2006. Ages 4–7.

Bullied by the powerful sun, the moon, personified by a Native American woman, gradually grows smaller and smaller until she completely disappears from the sky. Greatly missed by the animals on earth, she reconsiders her situation, and with help offered by a comet, returns a bit at a time to take her rightful place in the sky. This is a good example of a Native American *pourquoi* tale, a story that explains the magical origins of something, usually related to the natural world. An appended note that parents may want to share fills in background and supplies Native American names for the moon.

I Took the Moon for a Walk

By Carolyn Curtis. Illustrated by Alison Jay. Barefoot Books, 2004. Ages 4–7.

Here's a quiet contemplative collection of poems to read before turning out the lights. A boy reaches up into the sky, grasps the moon by its outstretched hand, and proceeds to go on a walk around his quiet neighborhood, the moon in tow, flowing along like "a summer kite." His travels, really more a series of lovely images than a story in the traditional sense, link to lulling four-line rhymes, each of which ends with the book's title: "I took the moon for a walk."

If I Had a Dragon

By Amanda Ellery. Illustrated by Tom Ellery. Simon & Schuster, 2006. Ages 4–6.

To make playing with his little brother more interesting, Morton imagines he is playing with a dragon. Unfortunately, even dragon playmates leave something to be desired. Morgan doesn't have a chance at scoring points when his opponent is as tall as the basket; dragons are too big to go to movies; and a dragon's fiery breath can singe a kid's hair if he's not careful. It could be that younger brothers, even if they're a little boring, make better playmates after all.

I'm Bad!

By Kate McMullan. Illustrated by Jim McMullan. Joanna Cotler, 2008. Ages 4–6.

Children familiar with the author-illustrator team's grumpy garbage truck (*I Stink!*), boastful backhoe (*I'm Dirty!*), and sturdy tugboat (*I'm Mighty!*) will have just as much fun with their born-to-be-bad T. rex, who boasts about his fetid breath and gnashing teeth. Unfortunately, neither of those assets does the snarly beast much good when it comes to catching dinner. His mom still has to help.

It's a Secret!

By John Burningham. Illustrated by the author. Candlewick, 2009. Ages 4–6.

Marie Elaine wonders where cats go at night, so she follows Malcolm right through his cat door and accompanies him on his evening ramble. Danger lurks (dogs), and climbing over rooftops isn't too safe either. But there's also dancing, and Marie Elaine, dressed in her diaphanous fairy costume, is perfectly attired for the evening's festivities. Perhaps it's all a dream. Kids will have to wait until the end to find out.

Itty Bitty

By Cece Bell. Illustrated by the author. Candlewick, 2009. Ages 4–6.

Itty Bitty is a teeny-weeny dog looking for a place to live. Hidden among some daisies he finds a bone, from which he chews a door and a window. His house, however, still lacks what's needed to make it a home. So he hops into his walnut-size car and drives to the city, where he finds a giant department store. He makes his way to the "Teeny-Weeny" department, where he finds everything he needs. Soon he's ready to sit on his brand new itty-bitty sofa and read his brand-new itty-bitty book in his cozy, itty-bitty new home.

Little Night

By Yuyi Morales. Illustrated by the author. Neal Porter, 2007. Ages 4–6.

Day is ending. Mother Sky has filled a tub with falling stars and prepared a bedtime snack for her daughter, Little Night. But evening is Little Night's time to play, and she coaxes her mother into a game of hide-and-seek that lasts until night wraps them in a blanket of twinkling stars. Lush language and brilliantly colored scenes of sunset and starlight will carry little listeners off to a sweet land of dreams.

Maybe a Bear Ate It!

By Robie H. Harris. Illustrated by Michael Emberley. Orchard, 2008. Ages 4–6.

In this version of a familiar scenario, the pictures tell most of the story, allowing little ones to add their own details. A whiskered critter clad in striped pajamas is ready for bed. He climbs among his blankets with his book and his stuffed toys—a bat, a shark, and a bear. He opens his book and reads, a look of total rapture on his face. But in the midst of a yawn, the book disappears! Chewing on his blankie, he mourns the loss. Has his book been stolen by a bat? Swallowed by a shark? Eaten by a bear? Eventually the lost is found, after which the critter gleefully skips across an empty white expanse with book in hand. The pictures are priceless.

Museum Trip

By Barbara Lehman. Illustrated by the author. Houghton Mifflin, 2006. Ages 4–7.

A class trip to an art museum affords an imaginative young boy the opportunity for a very special adventure. Having drifted away from his classmates to look at the art, he finds himself lost in the gallery. While searching for the others, he comes upon a display of maze drawings . . . and steps in. Following various twisting paths he finally reaches a castle at the heart of the maze and is rewarded with a medal for his perseverance. Back in the real world, he locates his class. As he leaves with the other students, sharp-eyed kids following the story will see that the boy still has his medal, a tantalizing suggestion that the trip may not have been a dream after all. The pictures demand close attention, but it's worth it.

My Garden

By Kevin Henkes, Illustrated by the author. Greenwillow, 2010. Ages 4–6.

After helping her mother work in the family garden, a little girl imagines what a garden of her own would be like. There would be no need for weeding, of course. And no garden of hers would have carrots. Her tomatoes would be gigantic, though, and her garden would certainly have a jelly bean bush. Chocolate rabbits would have no desire to eat her lettuce, and her flowers would bloom forever and ever. What a lovely exercise in make-believe.

Perfect Square

By Michael Hall. Illustrated by the author. Greenwillow, 2011. Ages 4–7.

By manipulating a simple square into a variety of surprising and beautiful shapes, Hall presents *creation* as both a basic process and a sophisticated idea. On Monday a square is cut into strips that are transformed into a lovely fountain. On Tuesday the pieces of a square beget a flower garden, and so on. When Sunday rolls around, however, the familiar routine changes. The square makes itself "into a window" and looks out on the creations of the previous six days. Have scissors and some precut squares close at hand.

Princess Hyacinth (the Surprising Tale of a Girl Who Floated)

By Florence Parry Heide. Illustrated by Lane Smith. Schwartz & Wade, 2009. Ages 4–6.

"Princess Hyacinth has a problem." She floats. To keep her earthbound, the king and queen put pebbles in her socks and have encrusted her crown with heavy gems. An encounter with a balloon man provides her the opportunity she longs for. After shedding her heavy clothes, she grabs a balloon and blissfully soars into the sky, the balloon string keeping her delicately tethered to the ground.

The Sandman

By Ralph Fletcher. Illustrated by Richard Cowdrey. Holt, 2008. Ages 4–6.

Not matter how hard he tries, tiny Tor, a dapper elderly gentleman, can't fall asleep. One day while journeying through the woods, he comes upon a dragon's scale, which, when ground into powder, induces sleep. Traveling around in his mouse-drawn cart with button wheels, he sprinkles his magic dust on children not quite ready to let go of the events of the day. All too soon, his supply runs out, and to replenish it he must steal a scale from the fire-breathing beast. Kids will pore over the items in Tor's miniature world and thrill to the gentle gent's bravery as he confronts the dragon on behalf of sleepless children everywhere.

The Shivers in the Fridge

By Fran Manushkin. Illustrated by Paul O. Zelinsky. Dutton, 2006. Ages 4–6.

It may take a minute or two for children to catch on, but once they do, they'll love the joke. Sonny Shivers and his family huddle together in a dark, precarious place. They are surrounded by strange-looking trees, pools of glistening red stuff, and clouds as sweet as cream. They are also very, very cold. If that isn't enough, every now and then there's an earthquake, light fills their space, and a monster (which looks very like a human hand) enters their world and takes something out (Jell-o, perhaps, or broccoli). Finally the Shiverses have had enough. One by one they venture out looking for a warmer, safer place to live. They find it on the refrigerator door—right where refrigerator magnets belong. There's something funny and fantastic on every page.

Sidewalk Circus

By Paul Fleischman. Illustrated by Kevin Hawkes. Candlewick, 2004. Ages 5–7.

The ordinary becomes extraordinary in this nearly wordless book, which begins when a child waiting for a bus spies a marquee advertising the arrival of the "World-Renowned Garibaldi Circus." In a wink, the child becomes a spectator at a big-top show, her imagination taking cues from circus fliers, banners, and playful shadows on the street. Construction workers on high beams become tightrope walkers; boys fooling around on skateboards become clowns; a chef flipping pancakes becomes a juggler. Step right up—the show is about to begin.

So Sleepy Story

By Uri Schulevitz. Illustrated by the author. Farrar Straus Giroux, 2006. Ages 4–6.

Put this book on the shelf right next to your copy of Margaret Wise Brown's *Goodnight Moon*. Though the situations are quite different, this tale, like Brown's classic, maintains a soothing rhythm that will lull little ones to sleep. The trees are fast asleep, the house is fast asleep, and a little boy, tucked in tight, is fast asleep. Suddenly, musical notes float through an open window, beckoning the child. He wakes, and accompanied by the tables, chairs, and other objects in his room, floats from his bed to enjoy a midnight dance. When the music ends, everything falls back into place, leaving the house oh so sleepy once again.

Stars

By Mary Lyn Ray. Illustrated by Marla Frazee. Beach Lane, 2011. Ages 4–6.

Imagination is at work on every page of this lovely, lyrical book that begins as children contemplate the way night becomes less scary when the stars come out. On subsequent pages children follow the stars—flying on sleds through snowflakes that twinkle like stars and watching fireworks spill starlike across the sky. They also discover how a star cut from paper can make them feel brave and make them feel safe. "Every night . . . Everywhere," children can follow the stars.

SuperHero ABC

By Bob McLeod. Illustrated by the author. HarperCollins, 2006. Ages 5–7.

Comics artist McLeod leaps into children's books with a comic-style abecedarian, which uses corny humor, alliteration, and comic conventions like word balloons to make learning a blast. Each of the characters has

Stars by Mary Lyn Ray

a superlative attribute: Rain-man uses rain to best villainous kids; Odor Officer keeps track of schoolyard farts; Skyboy and his sister don't walk home from school—they fly. Young preschoolers won't understand all the asides, but they'll be crazy about the high-octane, action-packed art and get the basic idea. Frank Cammuso's *Otto's Orange Day*, a story about a cat who loves the color orange, is a stellar example of how the graphic art form can be used to tell a more conventional cartoon picture book story.

The Toy Farmer

By Andrew T. Pelletier. Illustrated by Scott Nash. Dutton, 2007. Ages 4–7.

Rummaging around in an old toy box in the attic, Jed finds a small red tractor, driven by a tiny farmer with a pipe sticking out of his mouth. He shows his find to his father, who remembers playing with the toy as a child, calling it "the craziest toy he ever had." Not sure what his dad means, Jed carries on, playing happily with it until bedtime. When he wakes the next day, he gets an inkling of what his father meant: his bedroom rug has disappeared. In its place is a neatly plowed field. His subsequent journey into the farmer's world ultimately becomes a special secret shared by father and son.

The Weaver

By Thacher Hurd. Illustrated by Elisa Kleven. Farrar Straus Giroux, 2010. Ages 4–6.

Beyond the clouds, a magical weaver creates a beautiful tapestry that illustrates life as it unfolds on Earth. She begins her work in the morning, weaving pictures of people and the natural world in sunshine colors. As night approaches she chooses shades of blue and purple yarn to thread into her loom. At night, before she puts her work away, she covers Earth and all things on it with the brilliantly colored blanket she has made. A brief introductory note gives a few facts about the type of loom shown in the artwork.

Where's Walrus?

By Stephen Savage. Illustrated by the author. Scholastic, 2011. Ages 4–6.

While the zookeeper and other animals are napping, a walrus escapes. The zookeeper gives chase, but the walrus is clever. It hides in plain sight by ingeniously mimicking the people it encounters outside the zoo. Unlike Waldo in the Where's Waldo books, the walrus is easy to spot, whether he's posing with mannequins in a window display or dancing in a chorus line. The fun in this wordless book comes from seeing how the walrus blends in with the crowds and how long it takes the silly zookeeper to find him.

Willoughby & the Lion

By Greg Foley. Illustrated by the author. HarperCollins, 2009. Ages 5–7.

In this tale about a lonely boy and a lion, Foley goes one step beyond the usual story about a kid with an imaginary friend or a comfort object. Pictures, often simple ink sketches on white backgrounds, introduce Willoughby, coping with feelings about moving to a new home. The one good thing about it is the enchanted lion in the backyard. The lion offers the boy ten wishes, admonishing him to use them wisely. Adventures follow. The extraordinary experiences continue in *Willoughby & the Moon,* in which the boy discovers the moon in his closet.

Young Zeus

By G. Brian Karas. Illustrated by the author. Scholastic, 2010. Ages 4–7.

An enchanted goat named Amaltheia tells this story, which is largely faithful to the myth. It begins with Zeus's childhood and continues through his rescue of his mythological siblings and his tussles over which of them will take over the throne. There's energy, action, and plenty of humor in a story about superheroes and stupendous sibling rivalry.

9

THE NATURAL WORLD

I n his book *Last Child in the Woods* (Algonquin, 2005), Audubon medalist Richard Louv talks about children's increasing isolation from the natural world, a trend he views as detrimental to both their physical and emotional health. While acknowledging the power and promise of technological tools, he stresses that direct experience and environmental education are hugely important in developing vital real-world skills such as critical thinking and problem solving.

Books in this section are invitations to connect with the natural world. Some put their information into a fictional framework; some rely on sensory word images; still others let the intriguing facts stand on their own. What they all have in common is a respect for animals, plants, and other natural wonders, which aligns perfectly with a child's inherent curiosity. Reading them aloud can inspire children to explore the mysterious, fascinating places outside their front door.

Actual Size
By Steve Jenkins. Illustrated by the author. Houghton Mifflin, 2004. Ages 5–8.

Jenkins, well known for his extraordinary and beautiful paper-cut illustrations, employs them to excellent effect in this book of animal comparisons. Where book size might appear to limit the pool of actual-size candidates that could be included, Jenkins uses his 12-by-20-inch format to great effect. Tiny critters (a tarantula, a butterfly) fit comfortably on the page, while big ones like a tiger and a giant squid appear only in part. Children will have great fun envisioning the rest of the creature that belongs to the pictured piece; if they can't guess, a visual glossary of the animals appears at the end of the book. Being small in a big world is the stuff of kids' lives; this book, as Jenkins says, can help them "see how [they] measure up."

All the Water in the World

By George Ella Lyon. Illustrated by Katherine Tillotson. Atheneum, 2011. Ages 4–6.

Poetry studded with information and dazzling art makes the wonder of the water cycle accessible enough for preschoolers to appreciate. A poet and teacher who grew up in eastern Kentucky, Lyon brings an earthy sensibility to her text, which calls up the tempo of the natural world as it celebrates water's life-giving role.

The Apple-Pip Princess

By Jane Ray. Illustrated by the author. Candlewick, 2008. Ages 4–7.

Following the death of a beloved queen, a happy, once-lush kingdom becomes bleak and joyless. The elderly king, who sees his own death nearing, challenges his three lovely daughters to restore the kingdom. The first two build mighty structures of wood and metal, hoping to impress the villagers. The third, Serenity, fears she can't compete. But while looking through a box of treasures once collected by her mother, she finds a single apple seed. The sprouted seed inspires other folks to plant. In time the kingdom is transformed into a green paradise that all can enjoy, and Serenity becomes its wise queen. This original folktale offers multiple opportunities to connect children to the real world—whether the post-read conversation centers on conservation issues or on self-esteem.

The Apple Pie That Papa Baked

By Lauren Thompson. Illustrated by Jonathan Bean. Simon & Schuster, 2007. Ages 4–6.

The words are different, but children will recognize the familiar structure of "The House That Jack Built," which underlies this tribute to nature and to loving father-daughter relationships. As in the original "Jack," the ending of this old-fashioned tale comes first: a little girl holds up a perfect "pie that Papa baked." From there, the little girl conducts listeners on a backward journey through the history of the pie, beginning with the apples, "juicy and red," hanging on a tree whose roots were nourished by the earth, which was watered by rain, and so on. The final

All the Water in the World by George Ella Lyon

picture brings parent and child together to share the humble but ever-so-delicious dessert between themselves and among a host of animal friends.

Arabella Miller's Tiny Caterpillar

By Clare Jarrett. Illustrated by the author. Candlewick, 2008. Ages 4–7.

"Little Arabella Miller found a tiny caterpillar," begins the old nursery rhyme on which this book is based. Jarrett cleverly fleshes out the simple rhyme, creating an engaging and informative book about the life cycle of the butterfly. Arabella, fascinated by the fuzzy, striped caterpillar crawling on her hand, takes it home, makes a place for it in a shoe box, collects leaves for it to eat, and watches as it changes into a beautiful butterfly. The four stages of metamorphosis that Arabella patiently observes are concisely described on the last couple of pages of the book.

Babies in the Bayou

By Jim Arnosky. Illustrated by the author. Putnam, 2007. Ages 4–6.

It's hard to choose among Arnosky's nature books. He's written more than ninety of them for preschoolers and early grade children, ranging in subject from coyotes to parrotfish to prehistoric creatures. Many are award winners. In this one Arnosky conducts a satisfying tour of a distinctive American ecosystem, introducing a variety of animals that make their homes around the slow-running waterway at its heart. A mother alligator guards her babies; baby turtles hatch from a clutch of eggs; ducklings swim about; a mother raccoon and her babies hunt for food. As with all of Arnosky's books, there's a lot to look at, and just the right amount of fact to pique a young child's interest—even if bayou country is very far away. Preschoolers will also like Arnosky's 2011 book *At This Very Moment*, which compares what animals do during the day to how a child's day unfolds.

The Beeman

By Laurie Krebs. Illustrated by Valeria Cis. Barefoot Books, 2008. Ages 4–6.

What do beekeepers do? A grandfather tells his grandson all about their work and about honey production in a book that speaks to an unusual job, to some fascinating insects, and to a loving intergenerational relationship. Grandfather explains different types of bees, how honey is extracted from the hive, and how it ultimately ends up in Grandma's muffins. Several pages of straightforward information at the end deliver facts about bee colonies, beekeeping techniques and equipment, honey, pollination, and bee "dancing." To round it all out, there's a tempting recipe for muffins.

Birdsongs

By Betsy Franco. Illustrated by Steve Jenkins. Margaret K. McElderry, 2007. Ages 4–6.

Ten different birds "coo," "caw," "eyah," and "tat" their way through an ordinary day in this lovely book, filled with opportunities to enliven read-alouds. Most birds will be familiar to children—among them, robins, mourning doves, sparrows, chickadees, and ducks. Their pictures, created in Jenkins's signature cut-paper technique, are accompanied by a lyrical bit of text and the word representing the bird's song in larger, easy-to-read type. When day is nearly done, a mockingbird appears to mimic the other birdcalls, and a page of "Feathery Facts" will encourage children to find out more about their favorite singer. *Bees, Snails, & Peacock Tails*, also by Franco, introduces children to patterns and shapes in the natural world.

Chameleon, Chameleon
By Joy Cowley. Photos by Nic Bishop. Scholastic, 2005. Ages 4–6.

The team that created *Red-Eyed Tree Frog*, a stellar example of a science book for very young children, offers another stunning photo essay, this one featuring a panther chameleon, native to the tropical rainforests of Madagascar. Crisp, clear, full-color photos portray this reptile and its habitat as it navigates the hazards of its tropical home in search of food, carefully climbing down one tree and moving to another. The deceptively simple narrative draws children right in: "What's this? A scorpion! Watch out, chameleon! The scorpion's stinger is poisonous." The layout is very attractive, with the photos set against lime, yellow, and orange backgrounds that extend the flavor of the reptile's tropical home. Fascinating to look at and fun to read.

Castles, Caves, and Honeycombs
By Linda Ashman. Illustrated by Lauren Stringer. Harcourt, 2001. Ages 4–6.

"A silky web. / A sandy dune. / A room inside a warm cocoon." Ashman's pleasantly rhyming verse rolls off the tongue, evoking snug word pictures of animal homes. Her words work closely with Stringer's art, which takes children into airy nests, hollow logs, tiny shells, caves, and honeycombs, where children will see spiders, raccoons, birds, beavers, and other animals comfortably at home. A picture of children, snuggled safely in their own beds, completes this cozy vision of the place where the heart is.

Compost Stew
By Mary McKenna Siddals. Illustrated by Ashley Wolff. Tricycle, 2010. Ages 4–7.

In this clever blend of fiction and fact, four environmentally conscious young chefs use an alphabet's worth of ingredients to cook up some "compost stew." Instead of spoons and bowls, they use pitchforks and wheelbarrows, and their stew pot is a large compost bin. Into the pot, they throw the expected leavings—eggshells, bananas skins, and "coffee grounds / with filters, used." But they also add a few things that might even surprise adult readers—hair clippings and laundry lint. After filling their pot and moistening the ingredients with a garden hose, they take a long break—and "let it all rot / into Compost Stew."

Dinothesaurus: Prehistoric Poems and Paintings
By Douglas Florian. Illustrated by the author. Atheneum, 2009. Ages 5–7.

Florian uses poetry and humor born of the familiar to help young dinosaur enthusiasts remember identifying characteristics of their favorite critter. Did you know *Brachiosaurus* was longer than a tennis court? The author's wit extends to his quirky art: an iPod dangles from the neck of a *T. rex* skeleton, and *Spinosaurus,* "with spines like a solar panel," wears long, red flannel underwear. A "Glossarysaurus" adds more information. If your child wants more on the subject, Kathleen V. Kudlinski's *Boy Were We Wrong about the Dinosaurs!* and Elise Broach's *When Dinosaurs Came with Everything* are excellent—though both are written for slightly older children. Kudlinski's provides facts; Broach's is just plain fun. Florian's *Bow Wow Meow Meow* is another great selection of poems, this one humorously profiling wild cats and homebody dogs.

Dogs
By Emily Gravett. Illustrated by the author. Simon & Schuster, 2010. Ages 4–6.

Dog lovers young and old will find this ode to canines and a lesson on opposites hard to resist. "I love dogs," declares this book's unseen narrator, who gleefully expounds on the statement: "I love slow dogs," fast ones, big ones, small ones, good ones, naughty ones, and all in between. The pictures showcase doggy opposites in fetching poses: a Great Dane with paws gently encircling a Chihuahua; a fuzzy pooch, abundant hair flying all over the page, alongside a tiny, hairless dog wearing a sweater. In a comic finale the unseen narrator turns out to be—a cat.

Down, Down, Down: A Journey to the Bottom of the Sea
By Steve Jenkins. Illustrated by the author. HMH, 2009. Ages 5–8.

In a fact-rich text with striking paper-cut illustrations, Jenkins conducts a journey to the depths of the Pacific Ocean. A variety of creatures swim across backgrounds of deepening color. Children will recognize some of them—the sea turtle, for example—but relatively few kids will have seen a Portuguese man-of-war or a hagfish. While they examine the pictures, parents can relay the information, which, while fascinating, is more detailed than young preschoolers will likely sit still for. Older children, on the other hand, will be totally fascinated by this view of a world so different from their own.

Elephants of Africa

By Gail Gibbons. Illustrated by the author. Holiday House, 2008. Ages 5–7.

Although Gibbons has written picture books about jobs and holidays and a host of other topics, her specialty is books that introduce children to the biological sciences. Her favorite subjects are animals and plants, and she's written about hundreds of them. This book is typical of her work. It includes information about the elephant's physical characteristics, family life, habitat, and behavior, presenting it in language children can easily understand. Watercolor-and-ink illustrations show the elephants in families, finding food and water, and facing danger. Close-up insets show more detail.

Fabulous Fishes

By Susan Stockdale. Illustrated by the author. Peachtree, 2008. Ages 4–6.

Planning a visit to a museum/aquarium? Read this first. It's full of facts to prepare the way. "Shiny fish / spiny fish, / fish that hitch a ride." Rhyming couplets and bright acrylic illustrations introduce more than twenty colorful (mostly) saltwater fish—from the lanternfish, which lights the deep, and the mudskipper, which uses its front fins like little legs, to the remora, which piggybacks its way across the ocean attached to a larger fish or marine mammal. Children will have fun identifying the various fish they see in the pictures; some fish are easy to spot, but some are camouflaged. More information about the species pictured can be found in end notes.

First the Egg

By Laura Vaccaro Seeger. Illustrated by the author. Neal Porter, 2007. Ages 4–6.

Seeger delivers a string of surprises while setting up a pattern that shows how one thing evolves into something else. Thickly textured backgrounds provide visual energy for minimalist images that cleverly incorporate cutouts. "First the EGG," reads the text on the opening spread, which shows the egg through an appropriately shaped hole. When children flip the page, they'll find a fuzzy chick and its adult counterpart ("then the CHICKEN"). And so it goes for *frog, flower, butterfly, word* (which becomes a story), and *picture,* which pulls everything together by showing the chicken, flower, frog, and butterfly enjoying a beautiful day together.

First the Egg by Laura Vaccaro Seeger

Pages are sturdy enough to support poking fingers and repeated viewings, both of which are guaranteed.

The Grand Old Tree

By Mary Newell DePalma. Illustrated by the author. Arthur A. Levine Books, 2005. Ages 4–6.

Each spring, leaves and blossoms cover a "grand old tree." Later the fruit appears, which provides food for the animals. Seeds from the fruit scatter; some take root in the soil. Squirrels and birds build homes and play in the old tree's branches. In fall, red and gold leaves cover the tree, eventually falling and disappearing into the wind. Then the tree dies, but as it decomposes, it provides food and safety for other kinds of creatures. What's more, the seeds it scattered over the years are already growing into stately trees that become "just like the grand old tree."

Guess What Is Growing Inside This Egg
By Mia Posada. Illustrated by the author. Millbrook, 2007. Ages 4–6.

Interactive books like this one are a terrific way to impart information to very young children. On one page is a picture of eggs in a nest or in other natural surroundings. This is accompanied by several lines of rhyming description giving a clue to the title question: beneath its father's "feathered belly an egg is cozy and warm, / Safe from the Antarctic storm." On the next page is the answer in large print, plus another paragraph of explanation and a picture of the hatched babies: ducklings, spiders, turtles, and, of course, penguins. At the end is a fascinating double-page spread showing the eggs' actual size.

Hello, Bumblebee Bat
By Darrin Lunde. Illustrated by Patricia J. Wynne. Charlesbridge, 2007. Ages 4–6.

"My name is Bumblebee Bat," begins this invitation to fly with a tiny mammal, "small like a bee." Each left-hand page poses a question: "Bumblebee Bat, how do you see at night?" The bat answers with a simple explanation on the following page. Beginning each question with the bat's memorable name establishes a pleasing predictability that will easily draw listeners into the facts. Wynne, a scientific illustrator who works (as does Lunde) with the American Museum of Natural History, gives plenty of detail in her large-scale pictures, which show Bumblebee flying, feeding, and finally at rest in a cave. The last spread offers additional information about the smallest bat species in the world. A good book for parent-child sharing, this will also entice science-minded children who are just beginning to read on their own.

Hip-Pocket Papa
By Sandra Markle. Illustrated by Alan Marks. Charlesbridge, 2010. Ages 5–7.

As with seahorses and emperor penguins, the Australian hip-pocket frog papa is the parent that raises the kids. Markle's text follows a father frog through the process, from guarding the eggs to watching baby frogs set out on their own. After eggs hatch, the tadpoles wiggle up Dad's legs to pockets on his hips, where they remain safely while he searches for water and food to sustain them. As Markel relates the frog's story, she introduces other creatures who share the frog's habitat, identifying each and describing them all more fully in a glossary. In *Finding Home*, Markle tells the heartwarming tale, based on a true story, of a displaced koala and her joey who wandered into an Australian residential neighborhood.

Hook

By Ed Young. Illustrated by the author. Neal Porter, 2009. Ages 4–6.

A Native American boy finds what he thinks is a chicken egg and brings it home for a hen to nurture. What emerges is definitely not a chicken; its beak is curved, and its wings are strong. Mother Hen knows that Hook, as the bird is called, is meant for "a higher place" than a hay-strewn barnyard; she knows this chick is meant to fly. But who will teach him? After Hook's own attempts at flight fail, the boy takes Hook, who turns out to be an eagle, to a canyon, where the bird is able to soar. The power here is in the pictures, especially those of magnificent Hook with wings spread wide.

How Groundhog's Garden Grew

By Lynne Cherry. Illustrated by the author. Blue Sky Press, 2003. Ages 5–7.

When Squirrel catches Little Groundhog stealing vegetables from his garden, he decides to teach Little Groundhog how to grow them himself. Together they collect the seeds, store them until spring, plant them, and harvest them. The resulting garden is so lush that they are able to share what they've grown with the other animals in the neighborhood. Cherry intertwines the facts and vocabulary of gardening into an entertaining story, illustrated with a combination of pictures related to the tale and that convey information about the plants and animals that make an appearance in the story.

How Things Work in the Yard

By Lisa Campbell Ernst. Illustrated by the author. Blue Apple, 2011. Ages 4–6.

How does a sprinkler work? How do dandelions grow? What do ants do? Ernst asks and answers twenty-one different questions about ordinary things children see in their backyards. She devotes one double-page spread to each topic, presenting a few sentences of basic explanation along with multiple illustrations with further commentary. Squirrels and butterflies are among the subjects included in this pleasing book, which encourages children not only to ask questions but also to look closely around their own world. A companion, *How Things Work in the House*, covers items such as soap, toilets, scissors, and bananas.

How to Heal a Broken Wing

By Bob Graham. Illustrated by the author. Candlewick, 2008. Ages 4–6.

In an unnamed city a pigeon falls to the pavement, its wing broken. Busy grown-ups pass by the bird. What does a small, injured bird matter to them? But a little boy and his mother do stop, and they take the injured bird home. They care for it, hoping it will someday fly again—and in a heart-lifting climax, it does. A tender story that children will want to read again and again. *"The Trouble with Dogs . . ." Said Dad* and *"Let's Get a Pup!" Said Kate* show the Australian writer/illustrator's more comical side.

How Many Baby Pandas?

By Sandra Markle. Illustrated with photos. Walker, 2009. Ages 5–7.

Baby pandas, most from the China's Wolong Giant Panda Breeding Center, are the focus of this book, which provides counting practice while it takes a look at an endangered species. It begins with the birth of one panda, tiny, pink, and naked. Then more pandas are born, with photos tracking their development as they grow into cubs. Suddenly there are six; then there are eight. The final page shows sixteen cubs, an exceptional number to arrive during the course of a single year. Markle closes with more facts about pandas and some information on the breeding center. Follow up with Nick Dowson's *Tracks of a Panda*.

Hurry and the Monarch

By Antoine Ó Flatharta. Illustrated by Meilo So. Knopf, 2005. Ages 4–6.

Hurry, an old tortoise, slow and steady, strikes up a conversation with a monarch butterfly on her way from Canada to her winter home in Mexico. Life changes little for the tortoise as the seasons pass. In spring, the monarch returns, and Hurry watches as she lays her eggs on some milkweed, then flies away toward the end of her life. In spring Hurry is there to watch caterpillars emerge and see the cycle start again. On the endpapers, a map of North America shows the 2,000-mile route monarchs take to their winter home, and more information about these amazing insects is appended. Sam Swope's *Gotta Go! Gotta Go!* offers another glimpse of the monarch's remarkable stamina. In the *Monarch and Milkweed* poet Helen Frost pays equal attention to the butterfly and to the plants that nurture it, while Lois Ehlert shows colorful butterflies of different kinds in *Waiting for Wings*.

In the Trees, Honey Bees

By Lori Mortensen. Illustrated by Cris Arbo. Dawn, 2009. Ages 4–6.

From "Morning light, / Warm and bright" to "Chilly night, / Cluster tight," simple rhyming couplets and photo-realistic, full-bleed illustrations track the life and work of honeybees, with additional facts placed at the bottom of each page. Close-ups of the inside of a hive—where various kinds of bees dance, bring pollen, care for their queen, and feed larvae—help give young children a solid understanding of what bees do as well as why they should care about the tiny creatures.

Insect Detective

By Steve Voake. Illustrated by Charlotte Voake. Candlewick, 2010. Ages 4–6.

The cover of this book is a clear invitation to explore the outside world, and the words on the pages will further pique kids' curiosity: "Lift up a stone and you might see an earwig scuttle out." In similar fashion, Voake encourages children to look for moths, bees, caterpillars, beetles, and other insects, presenting just enough detail to help them understand a little bit about the habits of their quarry and recognize it when they see it. For the preschoolers who want photos of creepy crawlies instead of drawings, ask your librarian for a copy of Charlotte Guillain's *Bug Babies*, which has plenty of amazing pictures as well as a text appropriate for younger children.

An Island Grows

By Lola M. Schaefer. Illustrated by Cathie Felstead. Greenwillow, 2006. Ages 4–6.

Geology is an unusual subject for a picture book, but Schaefer manages not only to make it compelling but also accessible to preschoolers. "Magma glows. / Volcano blows. / Lava flows / and flows / and flows. / An island grows." Schaefer's text is quite brief, but it still gives children enough information to make clear how islands are born and how they gradually evolve into a community that supports people, other animals, and plants. An afterword describes the evolutionary process in more detail.

Leaf Man

By Lois Ehlert. Illustrated by the author. Harcourt, 2005. Ages 4–6.

"Leaf Man used to live near me," begins this whimsical invitation to go into the backyard or to the neighborhood park to collect fall leaves. Ehlert uses dozens of leaves in this book, artfully arranging them on the pages to create clever collages to suggest an assortment of familiar objects—chickens, carrots, and Leaf Man. With acorn eyes and maple-leaf head, Leaf Man floats across fields and forests and mountain, all shaped from different kinds of leaves. In her author's note, Ehlert talks about collecting leaves wherever she goes, and she includes a page showing the leaves she uses in the pictures, identifying each one so preschoolers will know what they find on their own leaf hunts. Ehlert is also the author of the award-winning picture book *Waiting for Wings*, which follows the life cycle of four different kinds of butterflies.

Leaves

By David Ezra Stein. Illustrated by the author. Putnam, 2007. Ages 4–6.

Young Bear lives on a tiny island, which he shares with flowers, butterflies, rabbits, squirrels, and some trees. He loves his life. One day he sees a leaf fall to the ground. What's going on? More leaves fall! He tries to stick them back on the branches, "but it was not the same." As he watches and worries, he grows sleepy. So he finds a cave, snuggles into a pile of leaves, and dreams away the winter. When he wakes he sees tiny leaves on the trees and joyfully bids them welcome. Use this tender story to open discussion about seasonal changes but also about animals that hibernate.

Looking Closely along the Shore

By Frank Serafini. Illustrated with photos by the author. Kids Can, 2008. Ages 5–7.

City kids won't be as likely as children who have visited the shore to guess the objects showcased in this guessing game. Even so they'll still enjoy this book; they'll have fun learning about something strange and new. A mysterious object appears in partial photo on one page. Children are asked to "look very closely. What do you see? A flower? A fossil? What could it be?" The next page shows the full photo of and supplies some facts about the sea star, coconut palm, mussel, sea anemone, or other seashore inhabitant. The book is part of a series, including *Looking Closely in the Rain Forest* and *Looking Closely around the Pond*.

National Geographic Little Kids First Big Book of Animals

By Catherine D. Hughes. Illustrated with photographs.
National Geographic, 2010. Ages 4–6.

Animals are a very popular subject among preschoolers, and this is a zoo in a book. It's also nicely designed for parent-child sharing, taking inspiration from *National Geographic Little Kids* magazine. Hughes has chosen thirty mostly familiar species and assembled the kinds of facts that will most interest young children (a zebra foal "can walk when it is only 20 minutes old"). The photos, numbering more than one hundred, are dazzling. They transport kids to grasslands, forests, deserts, and mountains around the world to meet butterflies, frogs, giraffes, lions, spiders, and more. The pictures are so appealing children will want to "read" this book on their own. *National Geographic Little Kids First Book of Why* and *National Geographic Little Kids First Book of Dinosaurs* follow the same format and are just as engaging as this book.

No One but You

By Douglas Wood. Illustrated by P. J. Lynch. Candlewick, 2011. Ages 4–6.

Wood and Lynch encourage children to use their senses to experience the small miracles of the natural world: the feel of walking barefoot in a rain puddle; the slurpy tickle of a puppy's tongue; the chatter of a squirrel high in a tree. "No one but you can listen with your ears to . . . wind in the pines." Soothing words pair smoothly with realistic pictures that make immediate connections between children and nature.

Ohio Thunder

By Denise Dowling Mortensen. Illustrated by Kate Kiesler. Clarion, 2006. Ages 4–6.

It's a hot, sunny day on an Ohio farm. Soon clouds gather, and the sky darkens. The wind blows, lightning strikes, hail beats down on the tall corn, and cows bend their heads against the pouring rain. Mortensen tells this story of a thunderstorm in concise rhyming verse that makes each shift in the weather a sensory experience. "Marble hail / pelting crops. / Goosebump shiver, / icy drops," which all gives way to sunshine again as the storm passes through. Storm-shy kids will see that scary stuff eventually goes away.

Old Bear

By Kevin Henkes. Illustrated by the author. Greenwillow, 2008. Ages 4–6.

Snowflakes fall outside. "Old Bear slept and dreamed," then slept some more, dreaming whimsical dreams about all the wonderful things he experienced while he was awake. In his dreams, he looks forward to each season. In winter, the stars mingle playfully with snowflakes. In spring, a giant flower is his cozy bed. In summer, the sun is a daisy, and blueberries fall from the sky like rain. And in fall, red and yellow fish jump from the stream. When Old Bear finally wakes, he discovers a glorious new spring, with lots of new things waiting for him to explore.

Older Than the Stars

By Karen C. Fox, Illustrated by Nancy Davis. Charlesbridge, 2010. Ages 5–7.

In energetic yet informative language, Fox presents current theories about the origin of the universe. After pointing out, "You are as old as the universe itself," she explains how the universe evolved from a speck of cosmic dust, and follows the course of its evolution through the formation of our sun and the Earth. Younger listeners may need help with terms such as *proton* and even *universe;* a glossary will equip adults with all the information they need to answer children's questions; and a timeline concisely visualizes the enormity of the idea. For a lovely look at our emotional connection to stars, read Mary Lyn Ray's joyous, contemplative *Stars.*

Pierre the Penguin: A True Story

By Jean Marzollo. Illustrated by Laura Regan. Sleeping Bear Press, 2010. Ages 4–7.

At the age of fourteen, a penguin named Pierre is transferred to an aquarium at the California Academy of Sciences museum to spend his last years. Unfortunately, he becomes ill. He recovers, but he has lost feathers on both his back and his chest, and although he is otherwise healthy, other penguins begin to shun him. Inspired by the raincoat occasionally worn by her dog, aquatic biologist Pam Schaller, who cares for Pierre, comes up with the idea of creating a wetsuit for him, like the protective suits worn by divers. With no more than a few lines per page, Marzollo tells Pierre's sweet story of illness and recovery, at the same time divulging a few secrets about what it's like to work in a museum.

Red Sings from Treetops: A Year in Colors

By Joyce Sidman. Illustrated by Pamela Zagarenski. Houghton Mifflin, 2009. Ages 4–6.

The colors of the changing seasons are a favorite topic for children's book writers, but poet Sidman's book approaches the subject in a fresh way. The colors she associates with the seasons aren't always those that come first to mind. Spring brings green buds, but red birds sing in the treetops as well, and in winter pink "prickles: / warm fingers / against cold cheeks." There's a color surprise on every beautifully illustrated page of verse.

Sea Horse: The Shyest Fish in the Sea

By Chris Butterworth. Illustrated by John Lawrence. Candlewick, 2006. Ages 4–7.

"Every day at sunrise, Sea Horse swims slowly off to meet his mate. They twist their tails together and twirl gently around, changing color until they match." This is only one of the amazing facts that Butterworth assembles in his investigation of a day in the life of one of the ocean's most curious creatures. Using Barbour's seahorse as his model, he explains physical attributes ("a head like a horse, a tail like a monkey"), habitat, behavior, reproduction, the role of the father in caring for the young, and how young develop. Pair this with Eric Carle's *Mr. Seahorse*.

Swirl by Swirl: Spirals in Nature

By Joyce Sidman. Illustrated by Beth Krommes. Houghton Mifflin, 2011. Ages 4–6.

Sidman, the author of *Red Sings from Treetops* (above), is known for looking at the natural world in unexpected ways. In this book, she explores a lovely shape that appears in both the plant and animal kingdom. One can see it in the snail, in the lady fern, in a ram's horns, in a spider's web, and in the ocean's waves. Even the copyright page is designed in a spiral form. Each section of concise, free-verse text opens with the words "a spiral," and then goes on to characterize the shape as strong, clever, growing, or reaching out. The pictures are precise and amazing; each animal and plant is clearly identified, and final pages provide more information for parents to share.

Time to Eat

By Steve Jenkins and Robin Page. Illustrated by Steve Jenkins. Houghton Mifflin, 2011. Ages 4–7.

Birds peck seeds, rabbits nibble carrots, and the family dog eats his dinner, sometimes without bothering to chew. But how do other animals eat? For that matter, what do they eat, and how do they find it? Ostriches eat rocks to help their digestion. Shrews must eat every few hours or they'll die; anacondas, which can open their jaws wide enough to accommodate a pig, digest their food so slowly they only eat a few times a year. The facts are fascinating, and there are more in an illustrated appendix. The author-illustrator team takes much the same approach in *Time to Sleep* and *Time for a Bath*. Older children able to handle books with more scientific details will like *What Do You Do with a Tail Like This?* and *How to Clean a Hippopotamus*.

Turtle, Turtle, Watch Out!

By April Pulley Sayre. Illustrated by Annie Patterson. Charlesbridge, 2009. Ages 5–7.

Using the title as a refrain, Sayre explains the various hazards a single sea turtle might encounter during its development from egg to mature egg layer. The book unfolds as a series of suspenseful encounters. Raccoons and herons eye the hatchling as a possible snack. Gulls and sharks and fisherman's nets threaten it in the water. Each time, the turtle, shown gradually increasing in size, escapes. The book sends a clear message to kids to think about animal survival away from the zoo or the barnyard.

Under the Snow
By Melissa Stewart. Illustrated by Constance R. Bergum. Peachtree, 2009. Ages 4–7.

The author of the A Place for . . . science book series explores various ways creatures cope when snow covers the ground. Ladybugs crowd together to keep warm; centipedes winter in rotting logs; frogs sink down in the mud; beavers retreat to their lodges. Some animals spend cold months frozen solid! An award-winning writer with numerous books to her credit, Stewart knows how to make the natural world seem both fascinating and fun.

Up, Up, and Away
By Ginger Wadsworth. Illustrated by Patricia J. Wynne. Charlesbridge, 2009. Ages 4–7.

From egg sac to egg laying and a new generation, the life and death of a garden spider is chronicled in simple text and detailed illustrations. Most of this story follows one spider, who escapes a variety of predators to find a safe haven in an old barn. Pictures show spiders close up and also how they negotiate the landscape by soaring along on silken threads. The concisely phrased text is just right for reading aloud ("Her legs tickle the tips of tulips / until the thread lifts her / up, up, and away with the warm wind"), and there's plenty of information to nurture a child's interest in observing spiders in their own backyard.

Vulture View
By April Pulley Sayre. Illustrated by Steve Jenkins. Henry Holt, 2007. Ages 4–7.

Sayre makes those carrion-eating turkey vultures seem a little more approachable as she describes them and the role they play in the natural world. Her text is playful and occasionally funny, conveying fascinating facts sure to elicit an occasional "Eeeew!" Vultures look for foods that "REEK." Cut-paper collages, which show the birds' pulpy faces and heavy gray beaks, are just detailed enough to allow kids to recognize the birds at the zoo or in the wild.

White Owl, Barn Owl
By Nicola Davies. Illustrated by Michael Foreman. Candlewick, 2007. Ages 5–7.

As in her previous titles, such as *Bat Loves the Night*, zoologist Davies pulls young kids into the animal world with an atmospheric story that is filled

Vulture View by April Pulley Sayre

with facts. A boy and his grandfather build a nest for a barn owl. They watch, and eventually they see an owl settle into the nest. Words in large type tell the fictional story; lines in a smaller type present facts about owls' body features, behavior, and nesting habits. A concluding note tells more about nesting boxes. The poetic, sensory words (the owl's feathers have a "velvety softness") are enhanced by realistic pictures that capture the boy's delight in the beautiful birds.

Wings

By Sneed B. Collard III. Illustrated by Robin Brickman. Charlesbridge, 2008. Ages 5–7.

Wings come in many shapes and sizes. Some are covered in feathers, some have scales, and some are so tiny they are hard to see. Collard gathers an impressive array of birds, fish, mammals, and insects whose wings are beautiful or unusual. Each picture is accompanied by a simple phrase in large type and a fairly detailed paragraph of additional information. The pictures, which show wings varied in shape, size, color, and even number, are amazing. They are sure to attract children, who will come away from the book knowing something about a subject they might not have thought about before.

Winter Trees
By Carole Gerber. Illustrated by Leslie Evans. Charlesbridge, 2008. Ages 4–7.

While walking through the woods on a snowy day, a young boy and his large yellow dog come across seven species of trees: sugar maple, American beech, paper birch, yellow poplar, bur oak, Eastern hemlock, and white spruce. The child recognizes "the egg shape of the maple tree; / the taller oval of the beech," and talks about other traits that help him identify each tree—the way the twigs and bark and needles look. Gerber's softly rhyming poetry is nicely matched by the pictures, which show the different shapes of the trees clearly outlined against a quiet, snowy landscape. The end matter includes more information as well as illustrations of each tree mentioned.

Yucky Worms
By Vivian French. Illustrated by Jessica Ahlberg. Candlewick, 2010. Ages 5–7.

Children are fascinated by the slimy creatures. That makes this a great choice for home sharing, especially after rain brings worms out of the saturated ground. "Yuck!" says a boy when his grandmother digs up a wiggly worm from the garden. He changes this mind, though, when Grandmother tells him about the worm's body, what it eats, how its movements loosen the soil, and how its waste products help plants grow. Ahlberg's pictures show worms at work both above and below ground, and she occasionally allows worms to speak for themselves in cartoon speech bubbles: "Nice and rotten. Just how I like it."

Zero Is the Leaves on the Tree
By Betsy Franco. Illustrated by Shino Arihara. Tricycle, 2009. Ages 5–7.

Franco puts an abstract concept into terms children can understand by linking it to familiar things in the natural world. The book follows the activities of four children, whose play during various seasons of the year is described in the sensory images that explore a variety of things that are zero: "the sound of snowflakes landing on your mitten," for example, or "the kites in the sky once the wind stops blowing." The idea that *nothing* can actually be *something* can be tough for some children to take in; this book will help them toward a better understanding.

10

READING ALONE

Children are eager to learn to read; but to transition successfully from an active listener to an active reader is hard work, and it's not accomplished on a timetable—no matter how anxious we are to see them succeed. Forcing preschoolers not developmentally ready to read might be setting them up to associate books with failure. Most children express an interest in reading on their own between the ages of four and six. By that time they have begun to sound out words and look at pictures in books for clues to a story. By listening to you speak and read aloud, they have developed a listening vocabulary, and when you point out various words you and your child encounter as you go about the day, you have helped your preschooler build a sight vocabulary. By this time children have also started to grasp the idea that the words people say aloud can be represented by symbols on a page. In addition, most are able to focus on groups of letters and can track words from left to right.

At this point, picture books may seem too babyish to children, even though those with minimal text and certain design characteristics work well for beginning readers. Kids can also sit through longer stories read aloud to them, though most children can't read them. The books in this section, just a brief sampling of what's available, are ideal for helping children brand new to reading develop self-confidence and skill. Vocabulary in these books is minimal; sentences are very short—usually no more than five or six words long and completed on a single page. The type is usually larger than usual, and the spacing between the lines generous, making tracking easier for the child. If you want to help your emerging reader, try reading the book aloud, pointing to each word as you say it. Then, turn over the story to your sidekick, but only if he has expressed an interest in reading it herself. If she gets stuck on a word, urge her to look at the accompanying picture for a clue. Unlike the illustrations in most picture books, which add to the story, the pictures in easy readers reproduce the action expressed in the words as closely as possible. Your librarian is well equipped to guide you and your child toward leveled readers, favorite topics, and picture books that match your child's interests and reading proficiency.

Benny and Penny in Just Pretend
By Geoffrey Hayes. Illustrated by the author. Toon Books, 2008.

A couple of cute mice star in this book, which offers the visual appeal of a comic with language that brand-new readers can handle. Benny, who loves playing pirates, thinks his little sister, Penny, is a pest. Her princess costume doesn't help. When he calls her dumb, she cries. When Penny defends them against a pesky dragonfly, big brother decides she's not a wimp after all. The story will be familiar to new readers—it's the substance of many picture books. What's fresh is the presentation. The sequencing is easy to grasp, the characters' body language conveys the emotional content of tale, and the very simple dialogue is neatly deposited in speech balloons. Benny and Penny have appeared in several other adventures, which grow gradually more complicated.

Big Pig and Little Pig
By David McPhail. Illustrated by the author. Harcourt, 2001.

It's very warm outside, and Big Pig and Little Pig are hot. A swimming pool sounds like a great idea, but they don't agree on how to make one. Big Pig grabs a shovel and begins; Little Pig hops on an earthmover. McPhail's vocabulary suits new readers perfectly, and he invests his pigs with tons of personality—which make an already funny story even funnier.

Biscuit Goes to School
By Alyssa Satin Capucilli. Illustrated by Pat Schories. HarperCollins, 2003.

Biscuit's young mistress is going to school. Naturally the little puppy wants to go, too. Everyone but Biscuit knows that's not allowed, and off he goes. Once he manages to get to school, there's still the matter of finding his little girl, which causes all kinds of delightful chaos. Each page features one or two simple sentences. The words are mostly one syllable, such as *dog,* and some may already be in a child's sight-word vocabulary.

Chicken Said, "Cluck!"

By Judyann Ackerman Grant. Illustrated by Sue Truesdell. HarperCollins, 2008.

Earl and Pearl are set on planting a pumpkin patch. Earl has a shovel and seeds with a big pumpkin pictured on the package. Chicken wants to help. Unfortunately, her main talent is driving Earl and Pearl to distraction. She eventually proves her value, however, when she issues a hearty "Cluck! Cluck! Cluck" to chase off a bunch of pesky seed-stealing grasshoppers. The text is appropriately simple, with more challenging words, like *chicken,* appearing several times to reinforce learning. The comical pictures fit snugly with the story: "Earl watered the seeds" accompanies a picture of the boy holding a watering can.

Max Spaniel: Dinosaur Hunt

By David Catrow. Illustrated by the author. Scholastic, 2009.

"My name is Max. / I am not a dog. / I am a great hunter. I love to hunt dinosaurs." Well, he *is* a dog, but he's a dog with a big imagination. Equipped with a bunch of junk he's found in the yard, he stands atop an old skateboard and pieces together a dinosaur. A striped orange cat looks on with gleeful skepticism as a hockey stick becomes a jaw, a trowel is adopted as a toenail, and a garden hose is turned into a tail. Max's diligence is rewarded when his finished product makes a move toward the cat. Catrow's slapstick characters are terrific, and his very simple deadpan text is ideal for beginning readers. The toughest word in the book is probably *dinosaur,* and it won't take kids already fascinated by the big critters very long to learn it.

Ducks Go Vroom

By Jane Kohuth. Illustrated by Viviana Garofoli. Random House, 2011.

Repetition is a large part of the charm of this easy reader, in which a family of ducks is on the fast track to a relative's house. Once there they undertake a variety of easily recognizable activities, each one related in a rhyme. They ring the bell: "Ding-Dong, Bing Bong!" They eat: "Ducks slurp. / Ducks burp!" And they generally make a terrible mess, which they, of course, clean up in the end. The playful nonsense, illustrated with cheerful art, is glorious fun.

My name is Max.
I am not a dog.

Max Spaniel: Dinosaur Hunt by David Catrow

Fish and Frog
By Michelle Knudsen. Illustrated by Valeria Petrone. Candlewick, 2005.

Knudsen's easy reader comprises four funny, eight-page books. Each begins with a brief summary of the story to come, meant for a parent to read to the child, and closes with guidelines for parents wanting to make their child's reading experience as successful as possible. Each brightly colored page is devoted to one simple idea expressed in very few words ("Fish swims down") and an accompanying picture (a purple, bobble-eyed fish doing what's mentioned). In the stories, Fish and Frog, two good friends, swim, make funny faces, and play. The book's small size is a good fit for small hands.

Gus Gets Scared
By Frank Remkiewicz. Illustrated by the author. Scholastic, 2010.

Dedicated to "any kids who have spent a whole night in a tent," this book reader series features little child rhino named Gus, who has a new tent. His cute, smiling face peeks out of it; he can't wait to spend the night there. His parents applaud his courage. Equipped with his sleeping bag and flashlight, he begins his campout . . . but it's really dark, and really cold, and really kinda creepy. Children will probably guess what's going to happen, but they'll still have fun reading the simple story to its cozy conclusion.

Little Mouse Gets Ready
By Jeff Smith. Illustrated by the author. Toon Books, 2009.

Smith, well known for his Bone graphic novel series, turns his attention to a comic for brand-new readers. Mama invites Little Mouse to come along to the barn, which is one of his favorite places. Before he can go, he must get dressed. With due care he lays out his clothes: his tiny blue jeans, his bright red shirt, his white socks, and his underpants (label in the back, of course). Then he begins to put everything on. It's a scene right from a child's experience, which Smith depicts with a wonderfully comic touch.

Loose Tooth
By Lola M. Schaefer. Illustrated by Sylvie Wickstrom. HarperCollins, 2004.

"It's loose! It's loose!" Every child knows the feeling, but Schaefer makes it funny. A little boy wiggles his loose tooth for everyone in the family, even the dog. His sister tells him to be patient. His brother grabs the pliers (he has two sizes). Children will recognize both the delight and the anxiety that is part of the process, as well as the relief and the subsequent annoyance when the tooth falls out, leaving a hole that the tongue can't seem to resist. Cheerful cartoonlike illustrations capture all the emotional ups and downs.

May I Please Have a Cookie?

By Jennifer Morris. Illustrated by the author. Scholastic, 2005.

Pudgy Alfie the alligator loves cookies. His mother is baking his favorite. But when he reaches out to grab one, Mama Alligator encourages him to "think of a better way" to get what he wants. He comes up with several ways to get a cookie (one involving a fake mustache), but Mama doesn't budge. He gets a big hug, though, when he realizes what he needs to say is please. A page of rhyming words at the end of the book provides some additional reading practice.

Mittens

By Lola M. Schaefer. Illustrated by Susan Kathleen Hartung. HarperCollins, 2007.

Words of one syllable, in generously sized type, dominate this story about a new pet. Aptly named because of its white paws, a tiny kitten tries to find a comfortable place for itself in its new home. The strangeness is overwhelming. After looking for a spot behind the television and under the sofa, he hides under the bed. When a boy named Nick coaxes him out, Mittens finds the ideal spot—right in Nick's arms. It's tough being tiny in a great big world; preschoolers know the feeling very well. *Follow Me, Mittens* continues the adventures of the adorable kitty.

Peanut and Pearl's Picnic Adventure

By Rebecca Kai Dotlich. Illustrated by R. W. Alley. HarperCollins, 2008.

Peanut and Pearl, two fuzzy animals, love hats, but they have very different tastes. Peanut likes cowboy hats, while Pearl prefers bonnets with flowers and feathers. Nor do they agree on the food they want to take on their picnic. When Peanut disappears, Pearl thinks he's lost. Peanut, on the other hand, is quite sure where he was the whole time.

Pedro's Burro

By Alyssa Satin Capucilli. Illustrated by Pau Estrada. HarperCollins, 2007.

Pedro and Papa need a new burro to help them. They go to the market looking for one, but there are a great many to choose from. How will they find one? Then Pedro feels a tug on his shirt. It's a burro in a fetching yellow hat. Pedro, Papa, and the mischievous burro have all found exactly what they were looking for.

Pigs Make Me Sneeze!

By Mo Willems. Illustrated by the author. Hyperion, 2009.

By the author of the Knuffle Bunny books, this book is a good example of the Elephant and Piggy easy reader series, which uses comics-style balloon dialogue to relate the story. Gerald the elephant can't stop sneezing. Could he be allergic to his happy-go-lucky best friend, Piggie? Oh no! After sneezing his way through a visit to Dr. Cat, he learns he just has a cold. But when he finds Piggie to tell him the good news, Piggie is doing some sneezing of his own. With nearly fifteen equally funny books in the series, new readers have a lot to keep them occupied. Next stop, Willems's *Don't Let the Pigeon Drive the Bus!*

Puppy Mudge Wants to Play

By Cynthia Rylant. Illustrated by Suçie Stevenson. Simon & Schuster, 2006.

Henry loves his big, slobbery dog, Mudge, which he's proved many times over in Rylant's long-running Henry and Mudge books for newly independent readers. In this book, Mudge is still a wiggly pup—and he still gets into all kinds of trouble doing puppy things (and has started to slobber). He grabs Henry's stuff and makes himself a general nuisance, insisting Henry stop what he's doing to play with him. Of course, the boy and the dog have a wonderful time. For another book about a pushy canine pal, get *Go Away, Dog* by Joan L. Nodset.

Scat, Cat!

By Alyssa Satin Capucilli. Illustrated by Paul Meisel. HarperCollins, 2010.

A little lost cat is looking for a home. On its travels it encounters a dog, a pigeon, some townsfolk, a bus driver, and others. Everyone it encounters tells it to "scat." Finally he falls asleep on someone's porch. The next morning he encounters a little boy. The boy "did not say, 'Scat, cat.'" Instead he puts down a bowl of cat food and invites the little striped cat to stay.

Splish, Splash!

By Sarah Weeks. Illustrated by Ashley Wolff. HarperCollins, 2000.

Chub, a tiny speckled green fish, has a great big tub. He enjoys splish-splashing around in it. But what about his friends? He's willing to share, and soon he's playing host to a bull, a snail, a giraffe, a snake, a cat (who wears a shower cap), an elephant, a hippo, a mouse, a horse, and a tiny bug. There's even room for tub toys. What a bathtub! "And they splish / and they splash, / and they splash / and they splish." A lively story for beginning readers, who can show off even more by naming all the different animals on the cover.

Turtle and Snake's Day at the Beach
By Kate Spohn. Illustrated by the author. Puffin, 2004.

Equipped with surfboards, shovels, and a beach umbrella, Turtle and Snake are off to the beach. They decide to enter a sand castle contest, and they build an impressive one. After that they go surfing. While they are gone the waves knock down their creation. They build another, which is also knocked down. Will they build a third? Pictures provide clues for some of the more difficult words (like *umbrella* and *shovel*), but there are also plenty of simple one-syllable words that children may even recognize.

RESOURCES

The books, organizations, and online sites in this section are only a few of the many resources to help parents further investigate read-aloud strategies and early literacy issues and locate great books to share with their children.

BOOKS

100 Best Books for Children
A Parent's Guide to Making the Right Choices
for Your Young Reader, Toddler to Preteen
Anita Silvey. Mariner, 2005.

Looking for classic literature? Silvey's list of one hundred "essential" titles, published prior to 2004, is a great place to begin the search, whether the object is a book for a baby or for an older child. Eden Ross Lipson's *The New York Times Parent's Guide to the Best Books for Children* is another excellent resource for classic titles.

A Family of Readers
The Book Lover's Guide to Children's
and Young Adult Literature
Roger Sutton and Martha V. Parravano. Candlewick, 2010.

In this collection you'll find essays and articles from children's books authors, illustrators, and the editors of *Horn Book Magazine*, which is one of the premier children's books review journals.

Great Books for Babies and Toddlers
Kathleen Odean. Ballantine, 2003.

Don't let the copyright date stop you from taking a look at this book. Many of Odean's suggestions (most published prior to 2000) are still in print and still great choices for sharing with infants and toddlers.

Picture Books for Children
Fiction, Folktales, and Poetry
Mary Northrup. American Library Association, 2012.

Northrup offers a choice selection of picture storybooks (poetry and folktales) published during the last decade, for children in kindergarten through third grade.

Picturing the World
Informational Picture Books for Children
Kathleen T. Isaacs. American Library Association, 2012.

It's not easy to find informational books for young children. Isaacs describes more than 250 titles for elementary school children, some of which can be shared with older preschoolers or used for family read-alouds.

Raising Bookworms
Getting Kids Reading for Pleasure and Empowerment
Emma Walton Hamilton. Beech Tree Books, 2009.

Hamilton has compiled a wealth of book-reading strategies for parents to use with infants and children right through the middle school years.

Reading Together
Everything You Need to Know to Raise a Child Who Loves to Read
Diane W. Frankenstein. Perigee, 2009.

Frankenstein discusses ways to talk to children about books, describing one hundred particularly good ones (preschool through high school) to get a conversation started.

ORGANIZATIONS

Association for Library Service to Children
www.ala.org/alsc/

A division of the American Library Association, ALSC sponsors the prestigious Newbery and Caldecott awards, which are selected by librarians to represent the single best-written and the single best-illustrated (respectively) book of the previous year. The division also sponsors an annual list of children's notable books, for preschoolers through age fourteen. These lists are available for free download. ALSC also maintains a blog accessible to parents (www.alsc.ala.org/blog/?cat=96).

International Board on Books for Young People
www.ibby.org

Organized in 1953, IBBY is devoted to "promote international understanding through books." Its membership includes parents as well as educators, book publishers, teachers, social workers, and others from more than seventy countries around the globe. Annotated IBBY Honor Lists, a biennial selection of the best international children literature (for age six and up), can be downloaded for free from the site.

International Reading Association
www.reading.org

In addition to their annual "Teachers' Choices Reading List" (www.reading.org/resources/booklists/teacherschoices.aspx), IRA offers a number of free-to-download publications especially for parents who want to help their child develop a lifelong interest in reading.

National Association for the Education of Young Children
www.naeyc.org

This nonprofit organization "supports families in early childhood education and parenting needs." It counts teachers, childcare providers, medical specialists, and parents among its membership.

National Science Teachers Association
www.nsta.org

NSTA is devoted largely to teachers for grades K–12, but its annual list, "Outstanding Science Trade Books for Students K–12" (www.nsta.org/publications/ostb/), is a great resource.

Reading Is Fundamental
www.rif.org

Dedicated to putting books in the hands of all children, RIF is the largest nonprofit literacy organization in the United States. Its home page provides links to book lists, articles, and activities that can be used at home or in a formal educational setting.

Zero to Three
National Center for Infants, Toddlers, and Families
www.zerotothree.org

This national nonprofit organization is dedicated to providing health, developmental, and early literacy information to "professionals, policymakers, and parents" who are working to improve the lives of the very young.

ONLINE RESOURCES

Bookends
http://bookends.booklistonline.com

Hosted by Booklist Online, (*Booklist* is the review journal of the American Library Association), this lively blog offers personalized perspectives on current, kid-tested titles for children from infancy through high school.

The Cooperative Children's Book Center
www.education.wisc.edu/ccbc/

The CCBC, a noncirculating research library, is part of the School of Education at the University of Wisconsin–Madison. It publishes CCBC Choices, an annual list of best books for children, which can be downloaded at no cost. It also maintains a book-related discussion forum open to the public, CCBC-Net (www.education.wisc.edu/ccbc/ccbc-net/default.asp).

Database of Award-Winning Children's Literature
www.dawcl.com

Reference librarian Lisa R. Bartel maintains this up-to-date, searchable database of award-winning titles. The database, which displays results of 102 different children's and young adult book awards, is searchable by author, title, ethnicity, genre, and more.

A Fuse #8 Production
blog.schoollibraryjournal.com/afuse8production

Children's librarian Elizabeth Bird oversees this blog, which features a review of the day, links to other reviews, and an extensive list her favorite "kidlit" bloggers.

I.N.K: Interesting Nonfiction for Kids

http://inkrethink.blogspot.com

Book reviews plus interviews and articles by and about some the best nonfiction writers working in children's publishing today.

Kidlitosphere Central

The Society of Bloggers in Children's and Young Adult Literature

www.kidlitosphere.org

This site hosts the Cybils: Children's and Young Adult Bloggers' Literary Awards (www.cybils.com), an annual list of books selected by discriminating bloggers—reviewers, librarians, teachers, and parents—who are devoted to books for young people.

Planet Esme

www.planetesme.com

Teacher and author Esmé Raji Codell brings her experience with children and love of literature together in a dynamic site with plenty of ideas to help link children to books.

Reading Rockets

www.readingrockets.org

Although this site is largely for teachers, it has a special parents' section and routinely runs reviews and articles of possible interest to parents and caregivers, including reading tips for parents in English, Spanish, and a number of other languages.

ILLUSTRATION CREDITS

Page 23. From *Little Chicken's Big Day*, by Jerry Davis and Katie Davis. Text copyright © 2011 by Jerry Davis. Illustration copyright © 2011 by Katie Davis. Reprinted by permission of Margaret K. McElderry Books, an imprint of Simon & Schuster Children's Publishing Division.

Page 32. From *All in a Day*, by Cynthia Rylant, with illustrations by Nikki McClure. Text copyright © 2009 by Cynthia Rylant. Illustration copyright © 2009 by Nikki McClure. Reprinted by permission of Abrams Books for Young Readers, an imprint of ABRAMS.

Page 34. From *Buster*, by Denise Fleming. Copyright © 2003 by Denise Fleming. All rights reserved. Reprinted by permission of Henry Holt and Company, LLC.

Page 38. From *I'll Be There*, by Ann Stott, with illustrations by Matt Phelan. Text copyright © 2011 by Ann Stott. Illustration copyright © 2011 by Matt Phelan. Reprinted by permission of Candlewick Press, Somerville, MA.

Page 42. From *No Two Alike*, by Keith Baker. Copyright © 2011 by Keith Baker. Reprinted by permission of Beach Lane Books, an imprint of Simon & Schuster Children's Publishing Division.

Page 57. From *Henry's First-Moon Birthday*, by Lenore Look, with illustrations by Yumi Heo. Text copyright © 2001 by Lenore Look. Illustration copyright © 2001 by Yumi Heo. Reprinted by permission of Atheneum Books for Young Readers, an imprint of Simon & Schuster Children's Publishing Division.

Page 63. From *Pecan Pie Baby*, by Jacqueline Woodson, with illustrations by Sophie Blackall. Text copyright © 2010 by Jacqueline Woodson. Illustration copyright © 2010 by Sophie Blackall. Reprinted by permission of G.P. Putnam's Sons, a division of Penguin Young Readers Group. Published by the Penguin Group.

Page 77. From *Waddles*, by David McPhail. Text and illustrations copyright © 2011 by David McPhail. Reprinted by permission of Abrams Books for Young Readers, an imprint of ABRAMS.

Page 87. From *The Butter Man*, by Elizabeth and Ali Alalou, with illustrations by Julie Klear Essakalli. Copyright © 2008 by Elizabeth and Ali Alalou. Illustration copyright © 2008 by Julie Klear Essakalli. Reprinted by permission of Charlesbridge Publishing, Inc.

Page 91. From *Monsoon Afternoon*, by Kashmira Sheth, with illustrations by Yoshiko Jaeggi. Text copyright © 2008 by Kashmira Sheth. Illustration copyright © 2008 by Yoshiko Jaeggi. Reprinted by permission of Peachtree Publishers.

Page 97. From *Bats at the Ballgame*, by Brian Lies. Copyright © 2010 by Brian Lies. Reprinted by permission of Houghton Mifflin Harcourt Publishing Company. All rights reserved.

Page 104. From *Pig Kahuna*, by Jennifer Sattler. Copyright © 2011 by Jennifer Sattler. Reprinted by permission of Bloomsbury Books for Young Readers.

Page 112. From *Flotsam*, by David Wiesner. Copyright © 2006 by David Wiesner. Reprinted by permission of Clarion Books, an imprint of Houghton Mifflin Harcourt Publishing Company. All rights reserved.

Page 119. From *Stars*, by Mary Lyn Ray, with illustrations by Marla Frazee. Text copyright © 2011 by Mary Lyn Ray. Illustration copyright © 2011 by Marla Frazee. Reprinted by permission of Beach Lane Books, an imprint of Simon & Schuster Children's Publishing Division.

Page 125. From *All the Water in the World*, by George Ella Lyon, with illustrations by Katherine Tillotson. Text copyright © 2011 by George Ella Lyon. Illustration copyright © 2011 by Katherine Tillotson. Reprinted by permission of Atheneum Books for Young Readers, a division of Simon & Schuster Children's Publishing Division.

Page 130. From *First the Egg*, by Laura Vaccaro Seeger. Copyright © 2007 by Laura Vaccaro Seeger. All rights reserved. A Neal Porter Book. Published by Roaring Brook Press, a division of Holtzbrinck Publishings Holding Limited Partnership.

Page 140. From *Vulture View*, by April Pulley Sayre, with illustrations by Steve Jenkins. Text copyright © 2007 by April Pulley Sayre. Illustration copyright © 2007 by Steve Jenkins. Reprinted by permission of Henry Holt & Company, LLC.

Page 146. From *Max Spaniel: Dinosaur Hunt*, by David Catrow. Copyright © 2009 by David Catrow. Reprinted by permission of Orchard Books, an imprint of Scholastic, Inc.

INDEX

Page numbers in italic indicate illustrations.